THE SECRETS OF GOD

AQ SID

First Published in 2022

Becomeshakespeare.com

One Point Six Technologies Pvt Ltd
119-123, 1st Floor, Building J2, B-Wing,
Wadala Truck Terminal, Wadala (East),
Mumbai 400022, Maharashtra, India
T: +91 8080226699

ISBN - 978-93-5610-184-5

Disclaimer – This work is based on research and facts. References are quoted from holy scriptures of all religions. There is no intention to hurt any religious feeling, faith or community.

Dedicated to,
My daughter Ayesha

Because she believed I will accomplish.

Prelude

Have you ever looked at the world below through the window of a flying plane? Have you seen the different parts of the earth?

Sometimes you see a long stretch of grey or yellowish mountains where no human ever dared tread. Or in some other stretches, long and never-ending green pastures or endless shape of blue or grey water in large oceans. But all of it, planned so meticulously that if humans had been the creators of Earth, they could not have done it so well. Neither could any scientific evolution have planned it the way it is.

If you believe in God, you may find a few interesting facts here. This research-oriented work will refresh and strengthen your belief in Him. If you are not a believer, this work will leave you thinking why you did not believe in God.

Acknowledgment

I was 24 years old when I started this work.

The British Council Library at Nariman Point, Bombay and the American Center Library at Churchgate, Bombay were the only reference sources used for this work.

I owe much to these two great libraries.

It took me 40 years to complete this work.

Contents

How did He plan it?

The first question that comes to a thinking mind is how and why did He plan it?

Did He plan it for His own pleasure? Did He plan this Universe and beyond for a reason? Why was Earth among all planets selected for humans? Are there any other creatures on any other planets? How did He create a Solar system, the sun, the planets and the earth? The Creations of God are plenty on earth and in our solar system. As for the creation of God, we have a few answers in religious scriptures. Old Testament tells us that He created it in six days and rested on the 7th day. Quran is more elaborate on this subject. Quran tells us that He created Heaven and earth in Six days and His one day of working is equal to thousand years for mankind. Thus, we can calculate that He created the entire Universe in six thousand years. That is what was believed for over 2 thousand years in in scientific theories. The scientific reasoning also tells us that entire Universe came into being with a Big Bang. The Big Bang theory is also revealed in Quran.

But here, let us have an analytical approach for His creation. How and why? 'How and why' are 2 chips of reasoning, that

God has already planted in human mind. So, let us work on these 2 platforms of reasoning to find the secrets of God.

The Universe and planets are continuously being explored by astronomers. Man has already stepped on Moon and reached up to the surface of Mars. The search for life on other planets, alien existence, water, oxygen or atmosphere conducive for living has not yielded any affirmation so far. The scientific explorations have discovered that planet earth is the only planet in our solar system gifted with the atmosphere conducive for life. If the entire Universe came into existence with a big bang, then why did life evolve only on earth? Or if the life on earth came through a scientific evolution, then why not on other planets at the same time? The Big Bang theory affirms that it was a huge mass that scattered in space with a bang. While the planets took shape in our Solar system, including earth, the scientific theories have no clue as to why atmosphere conducive for life occurred on planet earth only. Why not on other planets. Of course, there are vague explanations that each planet has its own atmosphere. But there is no scientific explanation from where that huge mass of soil, rocks occurred in space that split with a Big Bang. We have only this available knowledge that life developed on planet earth. The Creator of the Universe, the solar system, the sun and all planets has chosen only earth for life and mankind.

And the humanity called the Creator as God, the Almighty in awe and respect.

God has worked on a formula for His creation. He did not base it on science. Science is the creation of mankind. He based his creation on Mathematics. And this is the first Secret of God; that everything He created in our Solar system is based on Mathematics. And God taught Mathematics to mankind for further evolution, reasoning and research. There is ample evidence to believe that our Universe is functioning based on a mathematical formula. And He did so in His own way of programming numbers. Odd or evens, He did it in a set pattern. So, we have seven colors. We have seven continents and seven oceans on earth. And seven skies too? There are seven days in a week. Does He like odd numbers, particularly number seven? There are 24 hours in a day and sixty minutes in one hour and sixty seconds in one minute. There are 365 days in a year. There are 12 months in a year. All fixed and based on mathematics. Odd or even, the entire working is in numbers.

Who planned it so?

Was it Mankind, through science conception or based on an enlightenment from God Almighty Himself? Creation based on mathematics is an obvious belief. But creation has occurred much earlier than human perception of it. So, who did it? It is obvious that creation of entire universe is a planned work by Someone Who wanted it to be so and He did it. And He based it on Mathematics and numbers. All planets rotate on their axis across the sun for a fixed duration. And it has never changed. Who set the orbit of Sun, and planets to fixed hours? It cannot have developed on its own.

Let us study His creations.

First and foremost, the Sun, the most powerful and never-ending source of energy. It is so powerful, even ruthless that few among mankind worshiped it as God. There is no escaping from its merciless heat in the deserts and it is a blessing in winter mornings in other parts of the planet earth. These 2 distinctive features make Sun a unique creation. A source of great energy and life for mankind, Sun is but a small creation of God. It is shining in our galaxy non-stop, yet Sun is rendered helpless unless its rays fall on something. Sun does not create any light or energy in the blank space around planets until its rays strike a surface. So powerful and yet so helpless. Who could have planned it to be so?

For thousands of years, gases are burning on its surface and transporting energy for life on Earth and other planets. The 2 chips of how and why in human mind have already discovered the quantum of energy, burning of gases on it. Now it is a scientific reality but it has been planned to be so. Create the heat and energy on its surface and transport it through its rays. It takes 8 minutes for Sun's rays to reach the planet earth but during course of this journey, the heat and energy is not wasted enroute unless it strikes a surface. What a way of preserving a source of heat and energy!

Can this occur on its own because we believe in all creation based on scientific facts or is there Someone Who planned it that way? Compare it with the heating system in modern homes. Heat is created in a burner in basement and transported to the entire house. Before He created mankind, He had already created everything required for mankind.

Moon is another creation for the service of mankind. For scientists, it is a detached part of earth, rotating around it. It is illuminated when sun's rays fall upon it. This is an authenticated and verified scientific theory. But why did it happen so and who did desire it to be so? So accurately that it helped earlier generations to calculate the number of days in a month and remained a source of light in the dark nights. Can science plan it to be so? The question is left for a thinking mind.

Among His other creations for mankind are oceans and mountains. God alone knows what He created within oceans. But He created both oceans and mountains for mankind. Scientists have already discovered a lot about oceans and the evolution of mountains. But apparently, both are created for the benefit of mankind. Among mountains, we created resorts, used it for leisure and adventure. While religious scriptures describe its creation for balancing earth's rotation, mountains stand for the valor and safety of mankind. Mystery and secrets abound in the oceans, but a purpose is also clear. It was meant for supporting mankind. Oceans provide means of living to millions of mankind.

Whatever He created on earth is for the benefit of mankind. From trees to Animals, all His creation is for the benefit of mankind. For science and logic, man discovered all that is on earth and beneath it. But who created it and left the same for the discovery by mankind? Who created iron, gold and diamond within the earth? And why? All these creations are the phenomenal secrets of God. He created all that is in Universe, planets and on earth. If we look at the Solar system, we find that Earth is the best and beautiful planet among all. Well, scientists will argue that Earth is beautiful because it has water and oxygen that generated life on it. But the water and icebergs have been discovered on Mars too. Then why is it that only Earth is so beautiful? Because *Someone* planned it to be so. And He did it much ahead of His creation of Mankind. To a thinking mind, it is crystal clear that Solar system and Earth were planned for a purpose. *He* decorated earth as we will decorate our houses for an expected guest.

Then He turned to the creation of Mankind, His best yet. Now here we have 2 perceptions about the evolution of human life on earth. On one hand, we have scientific theories and on the other, the religious scriptures. And both are running parallel like a railway track, depicting years of evolution of mankind on earth. Since this work is planned on analytical basis, it is essential to examine both tracks.

The scientific track shows us what Charles Darwin's 1859 theory of evolution established. That this happened based on biology, the process by which organism change over time. But the nineteenth century modern study of human anatomy by Andreas Vesalius was more relevant to how the mankind was created. The study of cellular structure of tissues and organs. Even today, if we look at human anatomy from a scientific angle, the entire structure leaves us in awe, the way it was created.

It simply strengthens a belief that mankind was meticulously created by *Someone*.

Coming to the religious track, we have detailed descriptions from Old Testament, Bible, Quran and Rig Veda that Man was created by God. Let us examine the religious scriptures about the creation of Man.

According to Old Testament Bible, "And the LORD God formed man of the dust of the ground and breathed into his nostrils the breath of life; and man became a living soul. (Genesis 2:7)"

According to the Hinduism faith, Matsya Purana, sage Manu was the first man (and the first human) created by God.

Quran describes how God created Adam, "We created man out of dry clay from molded mud" (V15:26). Another Quran verse confirms that God created Man with His own hands, "The Lord said, "Satan, what prevented you from prostrating before what I have created with My own hands? (V 38:75).

So, we have clear descriptions of the creation of man in all religious scriptures. And undoubtedly that "man was created first". The question arises, *so how the woman was created?* The genetics of man and woman are different.

God is One.

Let us now discuss if there are multiple Gods or only One God?

The very concept of God varies among mankind as a matter of personal faith. Some believe there are many Gods working together. Some believe in Him as Father or Son. And some believe that He is the One God.

What are the signs for such beliefs? Much has already been revealed to mankind through religious scriptures. History tells us about Messengers of God who brought His message to mankind. We have noted in history that many sage men went up the mountains or into Jungles searching for God. And perhaps He met some of them or heard some of them or spoke to some of them.

But we need facts.

Let us look into historical facts. History tells us about many of His Messengers and Prophets. We read many stories about them. But we know for sure that Prophet Moses existed before Christ. History tells us that Moses was a living person , a designated king of among the people of Egypt. History also tells us that Moses took the slaves out of the kingdom of Pharaoh and later they became his followers. He settled these slaves in the valleys of Jordan. And history tells us that God spoke to Moses. And whatever He spoke to Moses, he spoke the same unto his people or followers. History tells us that Moses claimed God spoke to him. Moses never said that *many* Gods spoke to him or even 2 or 3 different Gods spoke to him. He said *God* spoke to him like a friend. The God speaking to Moses was not from a team of Gods. He was *the* God, the Creator as the followers named him. According to the Biblical and Torah belief, "God's commandments, the *mitzvot*, were actually uttered by God Himself, in audible, intelligible Hebrew words, the full text of which is contained in the Torah.

According to Quran, "God spoke directly unto Moses(V4:164). Thus, history tells us that the God of Moses was One. It was not a personal belief or assumption. It was a fact in history narrated for years by his people. Let us move on. Where did God spoke to Moses at first? Religious scriptures tell us that he met Him near the Olive tree on top of the mountain. Moses did not see Him but heard his heavy voice asking Him to come close. Moses was asked to remove his shoes. This is yet another secret of God revealed to us. God likes cleanliness. Otherwise, why did He ask Moses to remove his shoes and come close? A point is noted here. Cleanliness is a must for the proximity of God.

Moses always spoke to his people about what God spoke to him. We do not find a single fact in the history of Moses that there were multiple Gods speaking to him or the God speaking to him was a particular designated entity. For Moses, he was *the* God, the Creator and Owner of the entire Universe. And so, his followers believed. We read about Prophets and Messengers before Moses, but for us the history of Moses is more relevant and authenticated. It is a real history narrated by people who lived with Moses and survived him. And perhaps Moses revealed more attributions of God than any other mankind on earth because God spoke to him directly as a friend. And often secrets are shared by friends. Once Moses insisted that he wanted to see Him and God persisted that he cannot see him. Yet Moses insisted, so he was asked to look at the mountain and if he remains steadfast looking at it, he will see God. A lightening struck down and Moses fell on ground. He couldn't see anyone. To many, this incident is part of the Old Testament or Bible or Koran stories. But for a reasoning mind, it is part of the history Moses lived in. The history of Moses tells us that God is One.

The history of Moses also tells us that God first sent out a set of ten Rules and Regulations for mankind called as Ten Commandments of God. And these 10 Commandments were further reminded by predecessors of Moses. Jesus reminded his people about 10 Commandments God sent and people forgot about it. He repeated all Ten Commandments and followers of Jesus included them in scripture.

The Word of God was revealed to the Prophet Muhammad, compiled as Holy Koran. And surprisingly we find all 10 Commandments revealed in different chapters of Koran. So, we get another secret of God. He never changes his Rules or amended His laws. He set only Ten Commandments for mankind, "The Laws" He strictly wanted mankind to follow His set of laws. These "laws" were set at the time of Moses, repeated by Jesus and revealed again to Prophet Muhammad(. Did He cancel any of these Laws? A study of these 3 religions tells us that He did not repeal or amended any of these laws. What were added were the codes for better living and a good human society. Such as love for humanity and equality as preached by Jesus, Zakat(charity), daily 5 times prayers and fasting for Muslims.

The times of Jesus were also recorded in history. We also read stories of miracles performed by Jesus. But what we need to know is not about the belief, but about the history surrounding him and narrated by his followers, later saved as history. He was seen serving humanity. People will come and ask him for something, and he will say, by God's will it will be granted. He never said that *he* will grant it. A leper came to him and asked him for cure and he said, "have faith in God and you will be cured". A blind person came to Jesus and asked for sight and he said, "have faith in God and you will get the sight". He raised a dead son for a mother. In none of his actions, Jesus said or revealed that there were multiple Gods. He only spoke about One God and preached for One God. He never claimed that he was the Son of God or that God was his Father. This theory of Trinity is also mentioned in Koran but here we are working on facts and reasons for research. However, a verse in Koran strikes to reasoning. The God is asking Jesus, "did you preach Trinity among your followers" And Jesus answered, "You are the God, you should know these facts?" The question was asked when Jesus was paraded with the burden of cross on his body. What a question to Jesus and what an answer to God almighty by him. And what a time it was asked. In our daily life, when we come across such a situation it becomes a memory.

I was interviewing with Air India Bombay for a job and I was asked a question, "Are you Maharashtrian?" I replied, "Yes sir I am a Maharashtrian." The board member said to me, "You did not answer me in Marathi", I answered him back again in English that "Sir, you did not ask me in Marathi". We apply much reasoning to 'intellect' in daily life, same is required to explore the secrets of God. No research is done by religious scholars as to why the God asked Jesus this question and how Jesus affirmed his stand. However, the history fact remains that only after his period ended, did the followers of Jesus believe him to be the son of God. These historical facts, not beliefs, affirms for us that God is One only.

Apart from history, we also find some secrets of God from scriptures or traditions of other religions. Hinduism is world's oldest religious belief. Rig Vedas tell us that God is One, all sublime and powerful. We do not find a single shred from human history telling us that there were multiple Gods. Again, from Human history and not from beliefs.

Muhammad, as the Messenger of God is very well recorded in human history and his times are believed as recent history. He preached that "God is One" is the basis to the faith of Islam. If anyone says that "I witness God is One and Muhammad is His Messenger" he becomes a Muslim. It is concluded in such a simplicity. Muhammad wanted his followers to have a faith based on fact that God is only One. The Word of God revealed to him has much to speak about it and warns that the merciful and benevolent God will forgive all sins of mankind except *Shirk*. (*Shirk* in Arabic means belief in multiple Gods). In Koran, warning verses tells that God will punish, burn those committing *Shirk*. But again, this research work is based on history and facts, and not on beliefs. So, let us examine few facts from history of Moses and Jesus again. The people of Moses will come and relate to him mistakes and sins committed and ask for forgiveness by his God and Moses will pray for their forgiveness. The people of Jesus did same and Jesus said, "God will forgive you". The practice is prevalent even today and we see Christians go to the window of Bishop in a Church and confess their sins and Bishop prays for forgiveness. Hindus go for the Chardham Yatra and seek forgiveness. Muslims go for Hajj and believe their sins are washed out. Here point is, whom you are seeking forgiveness? God A or God B or God C? When a person is asking for forgiveness, he or she is seeking it from only One God. This chip to seek help from One God is already planted in human mind. So why think for multiple Gods? No one is recorded in human history as praying to a team of Gods for forgiveness or salvation.

Why God sent Messengers?

The history of mankind is full of records of Messengers of God.

In fact, few Messengers shaped the history of mankind. Yes, Prophet Moses, Jesus and Muhammad shaped the human history. Michael Hart in his world-famous book, *The 100: A Ranking of the Most Influential Persons in human History* have included Moses, Jesus and Muhammad among the most influential persons in history. He ranked Muhammed, the Messenger of God at number one, Jesus at number 3 and Moses at number 15 in his selection as the most influential persons in the history. History tells us that Messengers of God lived among people of their time and accomplished the missions assigned to them. The Messengers of God conveyed the Message about God and guided the people in their times.

But why were the messengers were sent among mankind? Why couldn't the angels carry forth His message directly to mankind? Why was there a need to do this through Messengers and how were the message was conveyed by each of them. If we research 'why and how' about the Messengers of God, we get a few more secrets about God almighty. Angels did bring the message of God to Messengers. So why did they not deliver it directly to mankind? Because God knew that a man among mankind could convey His message in a better way than an Angel who would be an alien among mankind. Thus, He chose Messengers among different nations at different times of the history of mankind. Some of the Messengers were recorded in history and many of them were not recorded. We have a list of few Messengers who lived in our societies and delivered the Message of God. In fact, if we study the history and roles of these Messengers in human societies, we may surmise that all of the Messengers were assigned a particular task or mission. At the same time, these Messengers enjoyed few miraculous powers that were witnessed by people of their times and recorded.

What was the role and mission of each Messenger? What were the miraculous powers bestowed to them? Why were the Messengers armed with miraculous powers? The assignments and roles of the Messengers of God who existed among mankind, also reflect a few secrets of God.

Prophet Abraham is considered as one of the earliest Messengers of God, one of the first to announce that God is One. He existed 2100 years BC, during the times of a ruler Nimrud who announced himself as God. So here we note that Abraham's mission was to counter the claim of Nimrud and guide people at that time and to proclaim that God is One. And how he accomplished his mission is already there in religious books written by scholars. Since this work is intended for research on secrets of God, we look into the history of Prophet Abraham. A miracle attached to the history of Prophet Abraham is that he was thrown into fire but the fire "cooled down" for him. We saved this miracle and proceed to the next Messenger of God.

The prophets of God performed miracles during their times. Either they were bestowed with miraculous powers or the miracles happened as the will of God. However, each miracle has a reason. Prophet Noah built an Arc and sailed in troubled waters. The fire was cooled for Abraham. Prophet David could shape and twist iron as wax. Prophet Solomon flew with his carpet over the air and reached a destination in less than 2 days. Prophet Jonah was swallowed by a large fish and remained alive in fish belly. Prophet Moses spoke to God directly. He also hit a rock with his staff and got water gushed out for his companions. Prophet Jesus healed a born blind and lepers. He gave life to the dead. Jesus also walked on water. Many miracles are attached with Prophet Jesus. Prophet Muhammad was said to have fed many of his hungry companions through a single pot. Prophet Muhammad is also reported to have traveled to outer space. What were the reasons behind these miracles of the Messengers of God? The God Almighty bestowed His prophets with miraculous powers, why? Did He want to impress the mankind? What was the reason? If we study the reasons behind each miracle of each Prophet of God, we understand many more of the secrets of God revealed.

Reason behind Miracles:

These miracles performed by God or through his Messengers were symbolic indications that a day will come when a man himself will perform these miracles. And it has been achieved.

Let us have a look at each miracle of Prophets as described in holy scriptures or history. Noah's Arc was an indication that man will sail on deep waters and make a living out of that. Today mankind has covered entire globe by ships and cruise lines. Fire was cooled for Prophet Abraham. Mankind has invented fire proof dresses for fire fighters and extinguished major fires throughout the world. Prophet David turned Iron rods like wax candles. Today Iron factories mold iron into many shapes. Prophet David spoke to birds. Today a man can speaks many languages. Prophet Jonah was alive in a fish belly for more than a week. Today, naval solders spend weeks in submarine under the water. Prophet Moses hit his staff on a rock and water gushed out. Today, mankind drills through rocks and extract drinking water. Prophet Jesus bestowed sight to a blind person by the will of God. Today surgeons can restore sight to a born blind person with someone's donated eyes. Prophet Jesus cured lepers. Today, leprosy and many contagious diseases have been isolated by mankind. Prophet Jesus also walked on water. Today we see this phenomenon in water skiing. Prophet Muhammad fed many of his companions through a single pot. Today we see many *Langars* feeding poor through a single pot. Prophet Muhammad's Night Journey to Heavens and return to earth was also a miracle. He rode a spaceship called Buraq from Jerusalem and reached Heavens(space) within seconds. Mankind has already stepped on the moon and space-travel itself is a reality.

Prophet Joseph was given the power to interpret the dreams and predict the forthcoming events. Today, meteorologist can predict weather, forthcoming storms much ahead of its happening.

All Prophets conveyed the message of God. And God wanted mankind to learn about the coming days. The humanity was shaped through a course of time as devised by God. Prophet Muhammad was the last Messenger of God and he was designated as the Seal of Prophethood. Truly, no prophet emerged after him because the human race is already enlightened. Did not we hear our elders say a day will come when we will be able to see each other while talking on phone. It has already happened.

Likes and dislikes of God Almighty.

This chapter will look into a relevant secret about the God. What He likes and what He does not like. The examples illustrated here are from the history of mankind as the well-known facts. Few quotes and historical facts from religious scriptures and practices of Messengers of God are also included for supporting a view. Let us first look into what He likes most among His creation, mankind.

Does He like a man or a woman to be very pious, religious? A good worshiper? Let us examine the known 'likes' of God.

What He likes most among mankind

Cleanliness:

Cleanliness is next to godliness.

A well-known saying that reflect the very first preference of what God likes most. In history this phrase was first recorded in a sermon by John Wesley in 1778. But in reality, the belief in God and concept of cleanliness was very ancient, found in Babylonian and Hebrew religious tracts to the modern threshold of Islam. The cleanliness is the first concept that emerges about His likes. Remember the old story about Prophet Moses? When He first spoke to him and asked him to come close, Moses was asked to remove his shoes. Since the shoes carry dirt and other impurities from the ground, it is considered as unclean. Many people will not wear shoes inside holy shrines, places of worship and homes. Jews remove shoes when the priestly blessing is given in traditional synagogues. Cleanliness is part of faith, said Prophet Muhammad. Muslim will never enter into mosques wearing shoes. For Muslims, washing hands and face is mandatory before each prayer. These religious practices are historical. But, how come these practices were adopted for worshipping God? How did the human mind know that God likes cleanliness? Is it just a matter of faith or does it have some historical significance? Or maybe because it was always preached by the Messengers of God?

Moses and Jews were given the understanding of the concept between cleanliness and uncleanliness. According to Jewish belief, Yahweh dwells among the holy of holies. The concept of Holiness affirms that God Himself is holiest and likes "holy" or clean among mankind. What is cleanness? A study of holy scriptures tells us how the mankind was guided for "purity" or cleanness. There are verses in Old Testament, repeated in Bible and again repeated in Quran. We need not to go into details of these verses in Holy scriptures, but we can consider few historical facts. Perhaps Prophet Moses was the first among Messengers who defined the laws of 'Purity" and "impurity". "Wash your hands before you eat", was the advice of Moses for his people. Jesus advised followers to take bath or wash feet before coming. Prophet Muhammad has set a pattern for clean habits. Just hour before his death, Prophet Muhammad reportedly asked his wife Ayesha to give him *Miswak* (toothbrush) and cleaned his teeth for more time than usual. The Messengers were guides for their people and they were guided by the Commands of God.

Moses also set an order on how 'Impurity' can be removed from life. The incident is reported in *Old Testament* (Exodus 32:21,24) and *Holy Quran* (7:148). When Moses went to Mount Sinai and returned after few weeks, and found his people worshiping a Golden Calf created by Magician Samri. He got angry and told his brother Aron that in order to remove that 'impurity' (calf), he will burn it and flow its ashes into river. Moses set an order that unclean and impure objects can be removed from earth in that manner.

Religious edicts against Menstruating women since ancient history reveal that women were considered unclean during menses cycle and were prohibited from religious and social activities. In Hinduism, world's oldest religion, menstruating women were not allowed near place of worship and in kitchens. In Judaism, a woman during menstruation is called "niddah" and banned from certain actions. In Islam, menstruating women are exempted from mandatory daily prayers and Ramadan fasting. However, there is no social taboo attached. Since Judaism, Christianity and Islam cover the faith of majority of humanity, the practices prescribed or inherited therein have the relationship with the Commands of God. Undoubtedly, cleanliness remains the first 'like' of God. There is an indirect warning to mankind for cleanliness in Quran. A verse says, "He hath set uncleanness upon those who have no sense." (Quran XI-100). This verse warns mankind that only mad persons are exempted from cleanliness.

The next in line of 'likes' of God, we see the concept of 'thankfulness'.

Thankfulness:

Much is said and believed since ancient times that God likes 'thankful'. The Divine religions, Judaism and Islam have plenty of verses in scriptures on this subject. We also find how much importance was attached to 'thankfulness' by all the Messengers of God. Jesus used to thank Lord for the food before eating it, Prophet Muhammad used to thank Lord after finishing his meal. Both, in their right practices, taught mankind to be thankful to the Creator. Moses also advised Jews to thank the Lord after meals. Prayers of Gratitude and thankfulness to God are included in Hindu scriptures as well. From religious practices and scriptures, it is clear that God likes 'thankfulness'.

Here, however a question raises. Does God like cleanliness and thankfulness for Himself? And the answer to this question reveals yet another secret of God to us. The concepts of cleanliness and thankfulness are good for mankind only. An expression of Gratitude in any form to anyone is a rewarding virtue.

Justice:

The third 'like' of God in line is "Justice". Yes, God likes to do justice and likes men and women who do justice. The subject of justice appears so strongly in the likes of God that I wish I could have placed it as the number one. Numerous verses in Holy scriptures tell us that God like those who do justice. When justice is done, it is a joy to the righteous but terror to evildoers. (Bible). "What does the Lord require of you but to do justice" (Bible). "Give justice to the weak and the fatherless;

maintain the right of the afflicted and the destitute," (Psalm 82:3) In Hinduism the concept of Justice is linked to Karma (deeds) and Dharma (faith). Hindus believe that good or bad Karma will bring justice.

Harvard Law School, one of *the most* prestigious institutions of its kind in the world, has posted a verse of the Holy Quran at the entrance of its faculty library that reads as, "O believers! Stand firm for justice as witnesses for Allah even if it is against yourselves, your parents, or close relatives. (Quran 4:135).

The concept of justice as liked by God was well recorded since ancient times. From King David, Augustus Caesar, Ashoka, Salauddin Ayubi to Mughal Emperor Akbar, history witnessed rulers or men of piety who upheld justice. Then there are judges known for holding justice above everything. History also tells us about corrupt judges who shun justice. Justice is synonym to judges. A general ruling applied that judges failing in their duties will fail in front of their Lord because justice is so close to God that at times, He is believed to be delivering it Himself. There are stories from scriptures. Jesus pursued justice. When he saw a woman stoned in public for adultery, he stopped it saying she can be hit only by a person who himself has not committed a crime. (John 8). What an historic judgement it was.

An example of fairness in justice by God himself is revealed in a Quranic verse that referred to the last hours of Jesus when he was paraded with cross in neck for his crucifixion. The verse reveals an interrogation of Jesus by God, when he is asked if he promoted Trinity (three Gods) during his mission as a

Prophet? And Jesus's answer to God set the best example of an argument in a trial. Jesus replied to God, *"If I used to say it, then Thou knewest it. Lo! Thou, only Thou art the Knower of Things Hidden."* (Quran 5:116).

This illustration shows how fair trial is important for justice. How important it is to uphold fairness by lawyers and judges in a trial for concluding justice. Hindu epic Ramayana begins with the story of Valmiki watching two birds, one killed by hunter and the other mourning the sudden death of her beloved. Valmiki feels the pain of other bird and curses the hunter. Valmiki's curse is the justice inherited in mankind. There is also an example of justice done by God Himself. The incident is recorded from the life of Islam's Prophet when he left for a *Night Journey* to Heavens from the city of Makkah. Angel Gabriel flew Prophet Muhammad from Makkah to Jerusalem where he rode his flight to Heavens. Why was Prophet Muhammad brought to Jerusalem before he flew to Heavens (outer space)? Why he was not given a non-stop flight from Makkah itself? Why his space flight, *Buraq*, a horse like animal with wings was waiting for him in Jerusalem? In fact, his *Night Journey* was planned by God Himself. So why did God plan Prophet's *Night Journey* via Jerusalem? By doing so, God almighty did justice to His last Prophet. All Biblical Prophets, from Abraham to Moses and Jesus, lived and worshiped One God in and around the surroundings of Jerusalem, the Holy Land. Islamic scholars mostly concluded that Prophet was brought to Jerusalem first so that he could lead a congregational prayer of all Prophets. The event, as narrated by Prophet reveals that before riding his space flight, Prophet did perform 2 Rakas of Salat on the rock of the Dome. So, he did a *Sajood* (prostration) in the Holy Land. And that was the justice done by God Himself. Since all Prophets worshiped God in Holy Land, He awarded that privilege to the last Prophet of Abrahamic faith. Prophet Muhammad's return flight was non-stop from Heavens to Makkah. For believers, the Prophet's *Night Journey* was a miracle when time was stopped on earth.

Holy scriptures of all religions have verses telling God likes justice and He is the supreme judge for the mankind. And this is also a reminder to Judges all over the world.

Worship:

Does God like the worship from mankind?

The men and women worshiping God in any form? There are different ways mankind worshiping God under different faiths. Islam mandated 5 times prayers and a month of fasting on believers. Whereas Christians make liturgical or personal prayers. Congregational prayers are held in Churches. Jews worship God at home 3 times in a day. Congregational prayers are held in Synagogue. It is generally conceived that God likes worship from mankind. All the Messengers of God did worship in their own ways. Prostration on earth was the earliest practice of worship which is still prevalent among Christians and Muslims.

The Messengers of God guided their people how they should worship God. From ancient times and references in Old

Testament we find worship to God was mostly reciting glory to the Lord. "Holy, holy, holy is the LORD Almighty; the whole earth is full of his glory." Worship to God is an act of dedication by the believer. We find references for worship to God in practices of Messengers. Jesus was reported to be a practicing Jew. He will not start eating unless he makes prayer to Lord. Prophet Muhammad always reminded his followers to pay Zakah (charity to poor) and observe prayers in time. "Observe Salat (prayers), observe Salat" he said repeatedly to his followers. Jesus said, 'You shall worship the Lord your God and Him only shall you serve.'

Worship to God as a duty is conceived by believers in God. But no evidence is recorded in human history that God wanted worship by mankind. The Messengers who guided their people in their times have conceived "worship" to God as the most likely 'return' for all His favors. "Trust me. Fear me. Remember me and I will remember you", these are lines we find in Bible and Quran. For centuries a common belief prevailed among believers of God that the one who is more pious, more devote and more worshiping is close to God. So simply it is implied or conceived that God likes worshiping men and women among mankind. However, it remains a vague conception. If we study closely the 'worship' strictures prescribed in Islam, 5 times prayers and 30 days of fasting are good for the benefit of believers. Prayers are time bound physical activity and fasting has it is own established medical values.

Good deeds:

There are, other 'likes' of God on record. "Good deeds" by believers are also in the list. In fact, good deeds are emphasized by God in holy scriptures. God likes those who do good work. And what is good work? It is a very broad-spectrum concept and covers many aspects of human life where good deeds are defined.

Doing something good for mankind is highly recommended. In Hinduism, the Rig Veda says, "The person who is always involved in good deeds experiences incessant divine happiness". In Quran, God says, I will reward the good work Myself. Quran has many verses telling us that God likes those who do good work. The best verse I find is, "Good deeds annul bad deeds". In Old Testament and Bible, we have been reminded same, "And let us not grow weary of doing good, for in due season we will reap, if we do not give up. (Galatians 6:9). An old example of doing good work is planting a tree whose fruits will be enjoyed by others. Benjamin Franklin discovered electricity in 18th century. In 1802, Humphry Davy invented the first electric light Thomas Edison invented light bulb in 1879. There are many likes of Franklin and Edison who did good work for mankind and earned the favor of their Lord. Their 'good' deeds have immensely benefited humanity. And their work defines the category of 'good deeds' that God likes most. Good deeds are not necessarily the acts of piety or righteousness. Good deeds are all such actions that contribute to the wellness of humanity. American President Donald Trump shall be remembered for expediting Covid 19 Vaccine research that provided relief to mankind from a dreaded Pandemic. On the other side, history shows us Genghis Khan and Adolf Hitler and few others like the duo who massacred millions of innocent human beings. They are obviously not on the 'good deed' side of the likes of God. Again, the fact about good and bad people in history reveal a secret of God that He loves those who care for mankind and do-good work for others.

Sacrifice:

The holy scriptures and religious practices also reveal another 'like' of God: Sacrifice.

Does God like sacrifice? It is a widely conceived belief that God likes sacrifice. Since ancient times, people in different religious faiths indulged in different ways offering sacrifice to God. There was an ancient practice of 'burnt' sacrifice of animal among Jews. In Old Testament there is reference that God commanded Israelites to offer sacrifice on various altar. The Vedic sacrifice, Yagna was an ancient practice in Hinduism. Animal sacrifice was also commemorated among Jews and Muslims towards the event when Prophet Abraham was asked by God to sacrifice his son. When Abraham obeyed the command of God and laid his son for slaughter, his son was replaced by a sheep. Millions of Muslim sacrifice animal during Hajj period. However, a verse in Quran tells that, "Neither the blood nor the flesh of animal reaches to God". It is the faith of person offering sacrifice that is judged by the God. If God likes sacrifice, it does not mean a sacrifice is done by slaughtering an animal only. There are many methods when a believer sacrifices for pleasing God.

The greatest example of sacrifice was set by Prophet Moses who was designed to be a king by ruling Pharaoh but he opted to be a slave leader and carried out the mission assigned to him by God. The characters of Prophets Moses, Jesus, Muhammad, known in history set guidelines for the followers and through them, God himself guided mankind.

A fasting Muslim keeps away from water and favorite food daily for a month. The fasting is prescribed in Islam and he or she is sacrificing the daily charm of life. A Muslim in a non-Muslim society will see fellow citizen eating and drinking. Yet he or she will control the urge and *that* is sacrifice. A Hindu man keeping his mouth shut for a pledge of 'silence fasting' for God is sacrificing his routine pleasantry. A personal pledge or sacrifice by the believer creates a sense of devotion, love and attachment and brings him close to God. A Sacrifice by believer definitely remains in line of 'likes' of God.

Charity:

God likes charity. Yes, we have edicts in religious scriptures that tell us that God like charity, alms giving. Jesus said sell your possessions and give to poor. Do not turn away from he who ask you(Bible). "God loves the giver (Bible)". Charity or alms, also called *Zakat* or *Sadaka* in Arabic, is obligatory in Islam. *'The example of those who spend their wealth in the way of Allah is like a seed of grain which grows seven spikes, in each spike is a hundred grains (Quran 2:26). Yet, in another verse in Quran believers are asked not to rebuke a beggar and politely turn him away if no alms is to be given. Daan is a Sanskrit word that connotes the virtues of charity in Hinduism.* Also, *Daan* is regarded as the cultivating generosity in Buddhism and Sikhism. History tells us stories of many generous persons who spent their entire wealth for the cause of God. From ancient Greek philanthropist, Herodes Atticus or Alfred Nobel to modern day American actress Angelina Jolie or Lebanese singer Amal Hijazi, the world has a long list of philanthropists who spent their time and money for the needful among the mankind. From where they got this passion for charity? They are Jews, Christians or Muslims, all believing that God likes Charity. Generosity, charity and alms giving shall remain in the list of 'likes' of God. However, Charity for building temples, mosques or churches shall not be included in line with charity for the needful of mankind. Charity as the 'like' of God remains for the welfare of mankind.

Fear and Trust:

Lastly, I would include 'Fear of God' and trust in God in the list of 'Likes' of God. Yes, God likes those who fear him most. In old Bible we have this verse, *"Great is His mercy toward those who fear Him."* (Psalm 103:11). In Quran, God says, *"We have commanded those who were given the Scripture before you and We command you to fear God"* (Quran 4:131).

Why would God Himself ask believers to fear Him? The answer to this question will reveals a secret of God what He desires most. If a believer will fear God, he or she will not indulge in any act harmful to the mankind. He or she will always be a good person. And this is exactly what God wants mankind to be. History tells us that Genghis Khan or Adolf Hitler and so many others like them, in human history did not fear God and indulged in genocides or mindless massacre. Killing innocent fellow human beings cannot be expected from those who fear God. So, asking mankind, to "Fear me" (Quran) is like putting a saddle on a horse.

Believers are also asked to "trust in God". Trust in God is also commanded in holy scriptures and teachings of all prophets of God. Trust in God is the basis of Islamic faith. "God loveth those who put their trust in Him (Quran 3:159). In real life how a believer shall put his or her trust in God? The was well described by Prophet Muhammad in a Hadith narrated by Al Tirmidhi, that once Muhammad saw a villager leaving his camel without tying it. The Prophet asked him, "Why don't you tie down your camel?" The villager answered, "I put my trust in Allah." The Prophet then advised, "Tie your camel first and then put your trust in Allah." This story from the life of Prophet of Islam suggests that precaution and judgement shall precede trust in God.

When people in need would come to Jesus and ask for the favors of God, Jesus would say, "Trust in God and you will get it." So he would get sight for the blind and cure a leaper from his disease. US currency has an inscription, "In God we trust". Originally it was suggested by a Pennsylvania clergyman and later, in 1956 President Eisenhower signed into law a bill declaring "In God we Trust" as the Nation's motto. The American currency has since ruled the world and remains as the most traded bill in terms of daily use in global markets. US currency with Trust in God inscription is a testimony that God has already blessed it and awarded supremacy over all other currencies.

When God first spoke to Prophet Moses and assigned him the mission of saving Israelites from Pharaoh, Moses wondered if he would be able to do that alone? God allowed him to keep his brother Aron and assured that He will be with him. Moses trusted God and embarked upon his mission.

Prophet Abraham was asked by God to leave his wife Hagar and son Ishmael in a desert in another country and Abraham obeyed the command of God and left them in a desert. This Biblical and Quranic story shows how Prophets trusted God and obeyed the commands. The prophets were all humans like any other person, yet their trust in God won accomplishments in their missions. At the same time, it is all evident that God likes those who put their trust in Him.

What God dislikes most?

The Bible has a list of God's 7 dislikes, namely: haughty eyes, a lying tongue, hands that kill the innocent, a heart that plots evil, feet that race to do wrong, a false witness who pours out lies, and a person who sows discord in a family.

"The boastful shall not stand before your eyes; you hate all evildoers." (Psalm 5:5). Another verse in Bible says, "God hates the wicked and the one who loves violence. (Psalm5:11).

Holy Quran has repeated small and meaningful verses that reflect the dislikes of God. *"Allah Loveth not wrong-doers"*. *"Allah Loveth not evil-doers"*. *"Allah loveth not aggressors"*. *"Allah loveth not the prodigals"* *"Allah loveth not proud."* "And never did we destroy the townships unless the folk thereof were evil-doers" (This is a thought-provoking verse, and it can be analyzed in the light of some historical natural calamities). A similar verse says, *"And how many a community have We destroyed that was thankless for its means of livelihood."* (Quran 28:59).

With above reference from Holy scriptures of Divine faiths, we can easily summarize the dislikes of God, namely evil, hatred, denial of justice, pride or crime against humanity. However, this work is based on analysis of facts from history and guidance from holy scriptures. Many secrets of God are revealed as both scriptures and facts are studied together. The list of God's dislikes is similar to His likes. And it can be arranged in order of analyzed preferences.

Proud or Boastful:

There is a warning in Quran, *"Walk not exultant on earth"*. God does not like a proud or conceited person. Bible tells us that Satan fell from the grace for his pride. Quran tells us that God asked all angels to prostrate Adam and all fell except *Iblis*, Satan who stood defiantly. He was not angel but a Jinn made of fire. He boasted saying, God, you made him out of clay and me out of fire. How can I bow to him? Satan was among few Angels close to God and fell from the grace as he boasted being made of fire. Jesus listed pride along with very terrible sins like wickedness, theft and murders.

In the early days of Islam in Medina, Prophet Muhammad was once told by his companions that some proud people wear long robes and visit Prophet's Mosque in arrogance. He noticed their proud display of their riches in their costly garments and arrogant mannerisms. He immediately announced that people should not wear such long draping robes and come to mosque. Prophet wanted to forbid arrogance and conceit of such people.

Believers in God have heard it from Prophets and seen it revealed in holy scriptures that God does not like pride or a proud person. But are there any facts in history indicating that Gd does not like proud people?

The stories of conceited persons date back to Old Testament story of Pharoah and Moses. Pharoah was so proud that he declared himself a God. He was drowned helplessly in the middle of the sea when he cried for forgiveness. His mortal remains are believed to be preserved as a token of a conceited person died so helplessly.

In old history we have the story of barbaric Genghis Khan. His empire was more than double the empire of Romans. Yet he wanted to rule the entire world. His name was a terror but, in the end, he died a helpless person. There are two conflicting version for his death. According to one theory, he died as he slipped from the back of his hose and his leg was entangled in the saddle. The racing horse pulled him along hitting his head on rocks. The second belief related his death in isolation from his family as he was infected with pneumonia. In either case his body was never found. In the end, he never achieved the respect of an emperor in his death.

In modern history, Alexander the Great, Napoleon Bonaparte and Adolf Hitler are known for their ambitious pride to conquer the world. When alive, they were most powerful and ruthless but when the end took over, they were helpless mortals. In the end they were most helpless and worthless. Alexander died at the age of 32. In his last days he was a mute person and could not speak for two weeks before his death. He struggled illness, fever and died of typhoid or Malaria. It was a helpless death for the person who dreamt to be the king of the world.

Napoleon Bonaparte whose empire stretched beyond Europe also died helplessly. He lost the power to British in the battle of Waterloo and he was sent in exile as a prisoner to the island of Saint Helene. Napoleon lived as prisoner for six years and died of stomach cancer. What an end for a person who said, impossible was not in his dictionary.

Adolf Hitler who trampled humanity under his feet and forced his people to recite, "Hail Hitler" greetings on all occasions died miserably. He shot himself through his mouth. When his body was found he was not given a funeral. His own people did not like him enough, to bury him on German land. His body was burnt and ashes scattered around. What a miserable end to a proud person who always told his fellow Germans that they were Aryans and superior to others.

The pride laced with ambition turns a successful person into an egoist. The pride, proud or conceit in a person is not approved by God. More examples in history also support this secret of God.

The great ship Titanic was built in 1912 and it sank in its maiden voyage on April 10, 1912. The makers of Titanic claimed in an advertisement in The Times that they had built a safest ship that "even God cannot sink". The oceans experts were baffled how could such a strong ship was damaged and sank just hitting an iceberg. The accident revealed a secret of God that He does not like proud or boastful.

Evil

Holy religious scriptures reveal that God does not like Hate, Sexual immorality, and Injustice. These subjects are known, preached, discussed and believed. Since this work is based on research to explore the secrets of God, we continue exploring and next in God's dislikes we find "Evil". God does not like "Evil" is a dislike comparable to 'proud' or conceit. Evil does not necessarily mean symbolic to Satan or Devil. Evil is everything that goes against the interests of humanity or harms mankind or contradicts the teachings of the Prophets of God.

God has created everything for a reason and He set regulations for mankind. Evil is an act that goes against such regulations. There are many such examples in history showing us how the evil acted in defiance of God. Few among mankind totally disregarded the fear of God and enacted heinous crimes against humanity. Adolf Hitler will not the forgiven by any sensible person for The Holocaust. He killed innocent Jews, old, young, women or even small children. Emperor Caligula, the 3rd emperor of the Roman empire was a similar evil person. He enjoyed watching his prisoners or innocent persons getting eaten alive by animals.

Russian czar Vlad Tepes, known as Vlad The Impaler, Prince of Wallachia enjoyed cutting off the breasts of women and forcing their husband to eat them. He pierced or impaled 20,000 men in the city of Amlas, burned children and asked mothers to eat their own children. Genghis Khan, the Mongol emperor razed many cities, killed innocents. He used to put hot metals into eyes and ears of innocent victims. Maximilien, the leader of French Revolution believed that killing was the best way of forgiving people. Idi Amin was called 'the butcher of Uganda'.

The list may go on. There are too many people reported in history who played evil in human society, and there were few who were not reported for their crimes against humanity. A few of them incurred the wrath of God in this world and were humiliated. Perhaps the fate of few other evildoers was not reported in history; however, an 'act of evil' in human society is not liked by God. An act of evil can be defined in a larger perspective. In simple words, an act of evil is always against the established tenets of God. The Prophets of God guided their people what God exactly wanted from mankind. An act of divergence in the guidance of Prophets also falls under the category of evil. The largest faction of Shiism in Islam also falls in this category. Islam was completed by Prophet Muhammad in his life time and a seal of approval was granted by God. The religion was sealed by none other but the God Himself, and there was no title of Sunni or Shia in Islam. A Quranic verse tells believers to call themselves, "Muslims". No where in Quran or in the guidance of Prophet we find the word Sunni or Shia. In fact, earlier scholars termed an addition or alternation in Islam as *Bidda,* an innovation and titled it as *Fitna* (evil). It was in early 1500 that Shah Ismail established his military rule in so called Sunni Iran and declared himself as the Imam, declared Shiism, his own innovation. Mughal emperor Akbar was also reported to have started his own religion, "Deen-e-Ilahi". Scholar at that time were either in awe with the emperor or acted in diplomacy of eschewing it. But Akbar's tryst in secularism was an innovation against the established practices of Islam. The innovation against the dictates of God or as the guidance of the prophets of God will fall under categories of Fitnah (evil). We can retain 'evil' or acts of evil in the dislikes of God.

Against Nature:

Many acts of mankind against the established rules of nature need a scrutiny. There appears a reason to believe that God does not like reversing the creation of nature. There is no need to take references from religious scriptures for this subject. Climate changes, sex changes, acts of homosexuality, bestiality, sodomy and similar phenomenon reflect a reality that God does not like, as these are against the nature.

Remember Christopher Reeve, the famous actor of Superman movies? The story of Christopher Reeve gives an angle to this subject. He played the role of a super power, a savior for humanity. He was tall, well built and most suited in a role that showed power beyond human reality. But in real life he met with an accident at the age of 42 that left Reeve paralyzed from the neck down and left him on a wheelchair for rest of his life. He died at the age of 52. But his personal disability could never deter him from contributing to the humanitarian cause. In 1999, he created a non-profit organization for the benefit of those living with a disability. Yet another strange case is that of Bollywood actor Sanjeev Kumar. The famous Indian actor won many awards and excelled in playing award winning older men roles. Ironically, he died young at the age of 47. Like actor Christopher Reeve, Sanjeev Kumar was also known for his gentleness. Neither Christopher Reeve as superman or actor Sanjeev Kumar playing the role of old men did indulge in any act against nature, but they appear as the symbols of contracting Nature.

Of His Creations:

God has created everything in this world, solar system, black holes and beyond. God is supreme Creator.

Those taking sides for a scientific creation of Universe argue on unsupported theories. The Big Bang is one such theory strongly upheld by supporters of scientific creation of Universe. However, the Big Bang theory finds its revelation in a religious scripture foretold much ahead of the time. It was propagated for a scientific reason. A Belgian Priest Georges Lemaitre propagated in 1920 that Universe expanded from a primordial atom and parted with a big bang. Scientist worked till 1930 and established this theory as most authentic with Edwin Hubble observations that galaxies are speeding away from us in all directions with abundance of light and microwave radiation all that could be result of a big bang. There is no other appealing scientific theory or discovery about creation of Universe than the Big Bang theory.

A close scrutiny of all religious scriptures revealed that a clear reference is available in Quranic verse that says, *"Do not those who deny the truth see that the heavens and the earth were joined together and that We then split them asunder? We have made every living thing out of water. (21:30)."*

The Oxford dictionary defines word 'asunder' as splitting something into pieces with a burst. The verse clearly reveal that Universe came into being with a powerful burst, like bursting of an atom with abundance of light and radiation. Quran was revealed to Prophet Muhammad 1400 years before the scientific propagation of Big Bang theory. That God sent many prophets to mankind all over the world and sent His own revelations through some of them for guidance and enhancing the knowledge among mankind.

It is this divine knowledge that often strikes the border of science and technology. This shows a secret of God of how He guided mankind for the development of science and technology.

According to NASA, the matter in Universe pulled out itself via gravity about 6 billion years after the Big Bang. We find in Old Testament that God created the earth and heavens in Six days and He rested on seventh Day. Quran tells us that God created the Heavens and earth in Six days. His one day of working is equal to one thousand years of the human count. That means God worked for 6 thousand years for creation of Universe by the mankind's count. If NASA is estimating 6 billion years, we have clear revelation in Old Testament that God worked for six days, and Quran says six thousand years.

This is yet another live secret of God that He wants mankind to explore. To understand the reasons for His revelations in all religious scriptures such as Old Testament, Quran or Vedas. The more we research, we discover more secrets of God.

What was the next God created? What is the best creation of God? A chain of planets orbiting in space? A beautiful planet called earth with green pastures, life supporting atmosphere, ravaging seas, water, hills and a security system that destroy any foreign matter that enters into the atmosphere of earth. And for whom God has created all that is on earth? And created earth so protected? The only answer that comes to mind that everything created on earth is for the service or benefit of mankind. So, most important creation of God is mankind. The first man He created. According to Hinduism, Brahma split himself into two to create a male and a female.

Old Testament tells us, *"And the LORD God formed man of the dust of the ground and breathed into his nostrils the breath of life; and man became a living soul."* The creation of man was repeated in Quran in similar words, *"He began the creation of man from clay; Then He made his seed from a draught of despised fluid; Then He fashioned him and breathed into him of His spirit; and appointed for you hearing and sight and hearth."* (32:7)

Is it not strange that two holy scriptures described the creation of man (Adam) in same narration? Quran also tells us that God created Adam with both of His hands, a verse not spoken about by Muslim scholars. *"God said, Satan what prevented you from prostrating yourself to which I have created with both My hands?"* (38:76). Here we is another secret of God revealed. That He created man with His own hands. Both Old Testament and

Quran confirm that God breathed His own into man made out ground clay.

So, there is something of God mingled into the person of a man. This is yet another secret of God revealed here. Man has been gifted something of God Himself. You need to search for something gifted into the personality of a man. Here we find a tool to do so. The Islamic faith speaks about 99 names of Allah (God). And if we carefully study these 99 names of God from Arabic script, we find that man has inherited or gifted for all the 99 qualities of God in his person. Let us examine few – Al Rahman, the gracious, Al Raheem the merciful, Al Malik the King, Al Jabbar the powerful, Al Musawwir the artist, Al Wakeel the advocate, Al Muhandis the engineer, Al Majid the noble, Al Qadir all powerful, Al Sultan the ruler and so on. The 99 names of God cover all the leading quality professions of a man. When God breathed His own as the soul for Adam, He knew for what He programmed Adam. The angels (Bible and Qurant) and Jinns (Quran) were made of fire and angels act like Robots while Jinn are defined in Islamic faith as another creation of God similar to mankind. Humans cannot see Jinn or Angels; similarly, Jinn cannot interfere with humans. There is a veil drawn between the two. Jinn are described in Quran. God created Jinn out of smokeless fire for reasons known to Him only. But Jinn are employed by God to carry out some tasks pertaining to mankind. Islamic scholar Moulana Waheeduddin Khan writes that while traveling in an airplane he was looking out of window and thinking what makes an airplane fly? The turbo engines or perhaps God has assigned a Jinn for such task? For running the routine of earth, there are many tasks beyond human capabilities and perception. It could be a purely religious belief that God assigned forces for that purpose.

Beauty of Creation:

God has created a very beautiful world for humanity. The earth stands alone in beauty and life among all the planets in our solar system.

Why is only earth beautiful and all other planets made of barren lands?

The scientific answer is presence of water on earth. Which made it beautiful and full of life. God already announced in scriptures that, *"He created life out of water"*. God is Creator of 'beauty' on earth. All creations on earth reflect a beauty of a thinking mind. There is a beauty in the lush green tree and it is more beautiful when all leaves drop in autumn. A barren tree is as beautiful as a green tree. A verse in Bible tells us, *"He has made everything beautiful in its time."* (3:11). The beauty of earth is spread all over it, amazing and soul filling. A verse in Quran urges, *"Travel in the land and see how He originated creation."* (29:20). This verse appropriately proves that if you want to see the beauty of creation of earth, you need to travel and see it for yourself. It also contradicts the famous saying that *"beauty is in the eye of the beholder"*.

From outer space earth appears a 'Blue world'. The scientific explanation suggests that water blocks the white radiation of sunlight and reflect it as blue. Since sea water is everywhere on earth, this radiation gives it a blue color. And so is the sky blue and our world fully has a blue color. The scientific explanation is based on human perception and understanding of color. So, color exists in all the different variations on earth. Who created color? There are 7 recognized colors on earth. This is another interesting secret of God that He created colors in 7 numbers. His creation is numerical and 7 is His favorite number in 'creation' formulae. The science has a very vague explanation for perception of color by human eyes and minds. In history, Aristotle was the first to have given a theory about colors, believing that colors were sent from heaven through a celestial ray of light. Aristotle's theory was replaced by English Physicist Isaac Newton in 1660 who experimented with sunlight and prisms. He showed that clear white light was composed of seven visible colors. Isaac Newton discovered that a single light from sun creates multiple colors. Modern science has a theory that colors are created in human mind by the electromagnetic radiation of a range of wavelengths that are visible to the eye.

The science has only provided possible reasons for the production of colors since colors are visible. The question remains why colors are always same for few phenomena? Why all plantation, vegetation, trees are always green? When snow fall occurs, it turns the entire land and objects as white within its range. The flames of a fire is always yellow. The color of blood is always red. The science also discovered that all 7 colors spread all over the earth are not seen on other planets. But in a rainbow, the combination of all 7 colors is also seen from the surface of other planets. Rainbow truly represents the 7 colors created by God. References for color are revealed in Old Testament and Bible. Red is related to the color of blood animal for sacrifice. Red is also indicated for the blood of Jesus Christ. Green for vegetation The Blue color was noticed by Moses and 70 elders who went with him to the Mount Sinai (Exodus 24:10) and described the pavement under the feet of God as the sky blue. Science has explored the creation of colors, but it could not establish why 7 colors are produced on planet earth only. And this fact leads to a secret of God, that He created colors for the beauty of His creations. He gave color to humanity as well. It is not known what was the color of the skin of Adam? Black or white? But the entire humanity is given the color of black or white. Why God has given 2 distinguishing colors to human skin? Is white superior to black or vice versa? There is no superiority of the color of skin but the beauty is added with the skin color of black or white. A verse in Quran supports this view, *"Black or white, all are equal in the sight of Lord"*. Prophet Muhammad was also quoted as saying in his last sermon that, *"There is no superiority of a white person over a black person or of a black person over a white person, except on the basis of personal piety and righteousness."*

The black and white color of the skin only adds to the beauty of humans. God has a reason for creating diversity in languages, color and appearances of mankind all over the world. Imagine if mankind were only black or only white? If only one language would have spoken all over the world? Then surely, we could have easily concluded that humanity developed out of a scientific fusion. As a good artist will pour out his heart and imagination on a canvas, God, the greatest of all artists, has created a beautiful world for the mankind.

What are the beautiful creations of the God? The answer is simple and convincing: that count is not possible for mankind. Yet, we can discuss few beautiful creations of God such as a woman or a rose or this world. A woman, black or white is undoubtedly the most beautiful creation of God for the comfort of a man. Yes, holy scriptures tell us that woman was created for the comfort of a man. According to a chapter of Genesis, Eve (woman) was created by God by taking her from the rib of Adam (man) to be his companion. We find similar verse in Quran, *"He it is who did create you from a single soul, and therefrom did make his mate that he might take rest in her."* (V 7:189). When God breathed all 99 traits of His own into creation of man and later created woman for his comfort, He added beauty unto her. This beauty is all over the personality of a woman. For centuries, poets, writers and philosophers have written volumes about the beauty of woman but very little is said about the Creator of this beauty.

There is a long list of known beautiful women from oldest history to the modern history, namely from Cleopatra to Marilyn Monroe, Grace Kelly or Elizabeth Taylor, all well-known who have attracted thousands of hearts. These beautiful women ruled the hearts and were widely regarded as the beauty icons in our history. There are many attractive and handsome men from history till modern times who similarly reigned thousands of hearts, but concept of beauty was always associated with women. A woman, black or white, tall or short, slim or fat, is a beautiful creation and a gift for a man. The protagonists of equality of man and woman always argue that what a man can do, a woman can do as well. Arguably it is true. However, we learn from Old Testament that, a woman was created from the rib of the man (Adam), she automatically inherited the qualities breathed into the man by God. But as a woman was only created from a body portion of a man, let us assume 20 percent of body of the man (Adam), she inherited only 20 percent of the 99 professional qualities breathed into the body of the man. This argument appears stronger for the physical and historical facts of achievements by women in various professions in comparison to a man. There were women warriors but they succeeded less than men warriors. The same applies in many other professions as well. Leaving aside the arguments for the equality of man and woman, the fact reigns supreme that a woman is the most beautiful creation of God for a man. The beauty of a woman is designed for the comfort of a man. The science could have valid reasons and analyses for the physical differences of the man and a woman. But the strength of a man and beauty of a woman is the secret of creation of God and not a scientific evolution.

The beautiful creations of God are pervading all over the world. The scenic beauty of landscapes, the ice on mountains, water falls, flowers, green pastures, birds and so many. God is the supreme Master of the creation of beauty.

His Re-creation:

Every living thing that God is creating, He *is re-creating*.

Plants, trees, water, or mankind, all living things have been re-created. This secret of God is visible, noticed and discussed. No scientific explanation is needed when leaves fell from a tree, leaving it barren and soon with spring, the leaves return to same branches. Water evaporates from seas or rivers and return to earth as rain. Science labels it as the cycle of life. But this fact needs a close scrutiny. This cycle of life is what God designed as 'creation and re-creation.'

This fact is also announced in all divine scriptures. Hindus believe that humans are in a cycle of death and rebirth called *samsara*. When a person dies, he takes a second birth according to his good or bad *Karma*.

Life after death or resurrection is mentioned in Bible. Jesus said, *"I am the resurrection and the life. Whoever believes in me, though he dies, yet shall he live."* (John 11:25). And he said to him, *"Truly, I say to you today, you will be with me in Paradise."* (Luke 23:43).

There is life after death and all divinely revealed religion preach that heaven or hell will be awarded after death as per the deeds of a person in this life. This topic of life after death is repeatedly dealt in Quran. In fact, we find 2 relevant verses in Quran announcing that a person is given a new life after death, a claim in line with the Hinduism faith. The 1st Quranic verse says, *"Thereof We created you, and thereunto We return you and thence We bring you forth a second time."* (V 20:55). In another verse, said in Quran *"And He it is Who gave you life, then He will cause you to die, and then will give you life again."* (V 22:66). These two verses from Quran are very subjective for life after death. Islamic scholars firmly believe the second life is that which God will award to a person after death and that will get him or her into Heaven or hell. But for obvious perception it is more than clear what the Quranic verse says that life is given after death again for a second time. That means there is 'second life' or the *'Purna Janam'* (rebirth) as Hindus believe.

Quran also tells us that *"Every soul will taste of death. Then unto US ye will be returned."* (V 29:57).   The dead will be raised, was also a major theme in Old Testament. The Bible promised that the Lord would personally come to earth one day and the dead would be raised. The Lord will set up His Kingdom and righteous would inherit the God's Kingdom. The conclusive evidence from holy scriptures points that there is rebirth, there is second life for every living thing including mankind

The cycle of life is another principle in line of working of God for all living creations. For all other creations, such as time, universe and planets the working principle is Mathematics. These two secrets of working of God coincide with major scientific theories. The science or the theories based on science are merely the media exploring the secrets of God. Nothing came into being on its own. A Power, a Supreme Power alone made it so.

Of His Distributions:

International Air Transportation Association (IATA) has divided entire globe into 3 traffic areas. TC1 is North America and Canada, TC2 is Africa, Middle East and Europe and TC3 is Asia and Australia. If we study carefully, God has already distributed his blessings all over the world in a well-planned phased manner. The blessing or bounties of God are coincidentally routed through same 3 traffic areas. Or we can say the distribution of blessing of God is also divided in parts of the world, but equally in each region though. From early days of mankind history till modern times, the distribution of God kept pouring in.

To begin with, we can start with area 1, North America and Canada. The natural resources are plenty for the prosperity of North America. Its fertile land, abundance of water and oil, mineral deposits, vast forests. With its inheritance of abundant of natural resources, North America has become the leader in the developed world. Its currency also rules the world markets. The supremacy of US currency over others is reigning for last so many years. And it has been carrying a bold declaration on all denomination bills that, "In God We Trust". No other currency in the world has this declaration for the sovereignty of God. There is also a popular prayer, "God bless America" based on belief that America is a land for all embracing and always standing for humanity. No other country in the world has kept its doors open for the shelter of humanity as America did for years.

Canada, another large country in the region is also gifted with 2 major natural resources; it's oil reserves and timber industry. But no natural resources were given in hand directly. It was left to mankind for exploration and utilization. And the distribution of blessing of God was not confined to Area 1. God sent it all over the world in some or other form. Nothing comes in hand unless you strive for it. The same rule was applied for the distribution of blessing of God. From early history till modern times, it was left to mankind to find it and take advantage. This is yet another secret of God.

We can examine few more regions for fact finding on this subject. After North America and Canada, we have Area 2 – Europe, Middle East and Africa. What was distributed in these regions? Europe was gifted with so many natural resources. These included wood, fertile land, plenty of water, natural gas, coal and iron. Two sources that helped Europe's economy and its inhabitants since ancient times were water and fish. These two gifts of God were major contributors for the self sufficiency in Europe. Civilization and education developed Europe faster. Education was gifted to the people of Europe and they, in turn gave it to the world. Expeditions from Europe discovered America and more regions. When the first verse of

Quran was revealed to Muhammad in 6th century, it asked his people to *"Read, read in the name of thy Lord."* (Quran). It was the first message for Arabs to get education. The message was sent when Europe was already under Roman model of education and civilization. We can surmise here that after water, fish, fertile land, minerals, education was also gifted to Europeans.

Next region, Middle East in Area 2 was underprivileged until 1938 when oil first struck in Saudi Arabia. What was the bounty of Lord given for Middle East? There was no water, no agrarian culture, no minerals or industries. Arabs mostly survived on herding and trading at home and with neighbor countries. Their life style was imbibed with simplicity. At times, most Arabs will have only dates in lunch or a piece of barley bread. If we study the life and living style of Arabs prior to 6th century A.D, we will wonder if Middle East region was spared from the bounty of God that we are exploring as a secret? It was not only Middle East but so many other regions were not gifted or the bounty of God was not explored by mankind in some regions. The God has distributed his mercy, benevolence and bounty in all parts of the world; however, it was up to the mankind to explore it and avail it.

An obvious observation of the early history of Middle East and its natural resources will show that the entire region was devoid of any source of economy and contained a very hard life for the inhabitants. But, in reality the gift of God was more rewarding for Arabs. It was not the oil boom. It was an honor that God bestowed on Arabs from 6th century onward.

The Arabs were not expert warriors like Greek and Romans at that time of history. But the 'fire of faith' led Arabs beyond Middle East. The Arabs badly lacked military expertise and ammunition, armors, yet they emerged as a force to reckon with. The Kingdom of Islam that was established by Prophet Muhammad in Madina, Saudi Arabia was soon a power that stood against Persian and Roman empires. The second Caliph of Islam, Umar ibn al Khattab won more battles beyond Middle East and entered into Europe. This was an honor by God for the humble Arabs that within few years of the light of Islam, they were a known as a conquering force entering close to France and defeating mighty armies. The Arab forces did not plunder or loot the territories they won. They simply established the just rule of God and did not acquire any wealth for personal comforts or built luxurious palaces for themselves.

Umar Ibn Khattab (634-644 CE), who was the first ruler to introduce treasury and taxation system in good governance was also known for his piety. A real-life recorded incident from the rule of Umar Khattab endorses this fact. An envoy of Roman empire was sent to Umar for negotiation. He arrived in the city of Medina and looked for the Palace of Caliph and he found none. When he asked a resident about Caliph Umar's residence, he was told he should be in the Prophet's Mosque. So, the Roman envoy went to mosque and asked for Umar. A Muslim guided him to the Umar who was sleeping in the courtyard of mosque on a rough mat. The envoy was stunned to see the ruler of an empire sleeping in a corner of the mosque like an ordinary Arab. He could not believe this was the man who defeated mighty Byzantine and Sassanid empires. And this was the honor Arabs won for themselves. The just conquerors and clean rulers. That was the real gift of God for Middle Eastern Arabs. The Arabs were destined to be conquerors. They emerged as a force to reckon with. Later history shows how the entire Europe combined forces in Crusades, beginning with late 11th century till 1291, the combined forces fought wars to contain Muslim wars of expansion. This was the real gift of God for the Nomads and trader Arabs. The oil boom starting in middle 19th century was only bonus of the reward God chose for them. The oil boom brought prosperity, wealth and all the luxury of life for Arabs.

The next and very vast region in Area 2 is Africa. What was the bounty and mercy of God gifted to Africa? It is commonly known that Africa was gifted the most precious stone and metal in the world. For years outside nations are digging and taking out precious diamonds and Gold from Africa. It is world's largest exporter of gold and diamonds. Currently Africa is producing more than half of the world's diamonds. Questions are raised that if Africa is so gifted with precious minerals why people in most countries in this continent are poor? There are known reasons. The diamond digging and grabbing by outsiders was going on for years. The Middle East would have met the same fate when oil was discovered and greedy westerners lured gullible Arab owners of the oil wells.

The countries in Africa were also gifted with other natural sources. A suitable climatic atmosphere, wild animals and surrounded by seas connecting it to the world. The continent of Africa borders Mediterranean Sea, Red sea, Atlantic Ocean and Indian Ocean. The African continent was also privileged to be the oldest inhabited continent on the earth. Humans and human ancestors have lived in Africa for more than 5 million years. Africa has other natural sources too such as plenty of woods, cocoa beans, and tropical fruits. Recently oil reserve discoveries have added to the economy of some African countries.

The next in distribution of the mercy of God were Asian countries in Area 3. These countries, namely China, Indian sub-continent and eastern part of Russia, all were privileged with good weather conditions, agrarian culture and minerals. Asia got immense wealth of minerals such as fuels, coals, petroleum and natural gas. The largest Asian coal producers are China and Russia, followed by India and few other countries. Indian sub-continent has largest agricultural land and food production was the oldest source of economy. Fixed and timely weather conditions also helped in food production since ancient times. Weather conditions also helped inhabitants live simple life. This region was given plenty of natural resources such as air, sunlight, soil, water, birds, animals, fish and plants and surrounding seas. All the sources helped keep the region as self-reliant.

As happened all over the world, some of the favors of God were retained by some and some were lost. But the distribution of God was fairly done for the entire mankind. God's many favors are mentioned in Bible. In Quran, these verses speak about the favors of God, *"And the earth hath He appointed for (His) creatures, wherein are fruit and sheathed palm-trees, husked grain and scented herb. Which is it, of the favors of your Lord, that ye deny?"* (V 55:10).

God created planet earth for mankind and everything therein is meant for humanity. God has distributed his bounty everywhere in some or other form and left a command for humanity, that immigrate to the spacious world, "Migrate to the world, the land of God is spacious....

The immigration to other countries was first suggested by God.

His Appearance:

How does God look like?

Perhaps this question has haunted generations of mankind who believed in God and worshipped Him. And perhaps this is the biggest secret of God. An unsolved mystery cemented within four walls of belief in God. For centuries man wandered in deep ravines searching for the presence of God. We have stories of Hindu sages wandering into forests and few claimed for having met the Almighty or heard Him in person. Hindus believe in the formless Absolute Reality as God, the Creator. Yet, practicing Hindus make idols and images of multiple Gods as Brahma, Vishnu, Shiva, and Ganesh. Hindus conceive the images of God in different forms, make idols and worship in devotion. The first divine laws revealed as 10 Commandments to humanity, God has commanded that mankind shall not make images or idols of Him.

In Old Testament, we learnt that Moses spoke with God "face to face" on Mount Horeb, but he could never see the physical form of God. Jesus revealed that "God is spirit," (John 4:24, NIV), so any human manifestation of God is not his true form. However, Christians believe that God became a man in the person of Jesus Christ., *"And the Word became flesh and dwelt among us."* (The Bible John 1:14).

Again, we have this reference in Old Testament (Genesis 16:9-13) that when Abraham left his wife Hagar and son in desert as commanded by God. As they were dying of thirst, the Angel of God appeared to Hagar to provide water for the survival of her and her young child The Angel of the Lord that appeared to Hagar was God Himself. *"The she called the name of the Lord who spoke to her, you are The God who Sees; for she said, 'Have I also here seen Him who sees me?"*

The Hagar story is also authenticated by the Prophet of Islam (quoted by Ibn Abbass) that Hagar and son Ismaeel were left in desert and when she ran for water between the hills of Safa and Marwa, an angel descended and he dug the earth with his heel and water flowed. The miracle water, *Zamzam* is still flowing from the well for centuries and Muslim pilgrims drink it and take home as well. It is never ending. Ibn Abbaas said, *Prophet added that had the Hagar not filled her water skin and controlled the water flow, it would have been flowing on the surface of earth.*

God is omnipresent.

He is everywhere and He can take any form beyond human perception. The Hindu sages or others who wandered in wilderness looking for God might have seen Him in some or other form, heard His guidance and quoted Him among their people. Religious scriptures show us striking similarities depicting about God and guide us for a perception of what could be the form of God. That God created Adam first. Quran tells us that God created Adam and breathed His own into him. Adam was assigned as Deputy to the God. Old Testament said God created Adam and breathed into his nostrils. Quran give more explicit perception of God for an understanding. *"God said, 'Satan what prevented you from prostrating yourself to what I created with both My hands' (V 38:75). "Everything will perish save His countenance"* (V28:88). Both verses reflect physical attributions of God in terms as 'both hands' and 'countenance'. Yet nobody could see God. Moses spoke directly with God and it was reported that he insisted on *seeing* Him.

God told Moses that he could see Him if he would be able to hold the mountain in view. A lightning struck the mountain and Moses fell down. Old Testament tells us that God appeared to King Solomon in a dream as a man. But scriptures also tell us that God is all powerful and He is far from the perception of mankind. In Exodus, God appeared in a burning bush, as a pillar of cloud by day, and as a pillar of fire by night. There is a similar detailed verse in Quran, *"God is the Light of the heavens and the earth. The similitude of His light is as a niche wherein is a lamp. The lamp is in a glass. The glass is as it were a shining star, kindled from a blessed tree, an olive neither of the East nor of the West, whose oil would almost glow forth (of itself) though no fire touched it. Light upon light, God guideth unto His light whom He will."* (V24:35).

Speaking about His form, God is all powerful and omnipresent everywhere. God is light of the universe. Power and light mainly represent the form of God. Since He is all powerful, He can adopt any form. May be at times, God appeared as a man for somebody or as an Angel for someone. In Christian theology, the incarnation is the belief that Jesus Christ is the second person of the Trinity, the son of God. The belief entails that Jesus is fully God and fully human. The miracles performed by Jesus, at a time when human perception was confined within belief only, were enough to engulf his companions in awe. But Jesus never said that he was the son of God or he was God himself. In fact, every time he performed a miracle, history quotes, not the religious belief, that he said. *'Believe in God and you will be cured.'* The miracles performed by Jesus led his companion believe that he was incarnation of God in human form. His companion, including St. Paul, who later compiled Bible and religion of Christianity, had seen his miracles and his love for humanity. These two were the attributes enough to lead a belief that Jesus was incarnation of God himself. Quran also refers to all his miracles, also about Jesus speaking to his people from his infantry cradle. The chapter Maryam in Quran details it as, *"Carrying her child, she (Mary), brought him to her people. They said, 'O Mary, you have indeed done something terrible! Sister of Aaron, your father was not an evil man, nor was your mother an unchaste woman!"*

She pointed to the child. They said, 'How shall we talk to someone who is a child in the cradle?' (But), he (Jesus) said, *"I am God's servant. He has given me the Book and made me a prophet; He has made me blessed wherever I may be and has enjoined upon me prayer and almsgiving throughout my life. He has made me dutiful toward my mother, and He has not made me arrogant or wicked.*

Blessed was I only the day I was born and blessed I shall be on the day I die, and, on the day, I am raised to life again." (V19:29-33).

There is another story I read in my childhood. A Hindu Sadhu went in wilderness searching for God. He spent years of his life in wandering in dark forests, walking by rivers or mountains. One fine morning, when the first ray of the sun gleamed on his face, he saw an old man coming slowly towards him. He was holding a beggar's cup in hand and looked very old. When he came close to Sadhu, he begged for alms. Sadhu admonished him showing his own empty cup. The beggar walked away and then the Sadhu noticed a gold coin in his empty cup. He threw the cup on earth and ran after the old man but did not see him anywhere. In despair he returned to take his cup again and noticed that the gold coin has gone too. Now the Sadhu firmly believed that he met with the God. If the gold coin would have remained in his pot, it would have been sent as a reward to him for all the best years of his life he spent in search of God. The coin was shown to him but the fact that it vanished meant that he achieved the desired goal.

Since God is all powerful, pervading and capable of taking any form anywhere, and it is beyond human perception to idolize Him or personify Him in any image, it is only logical we conclude God is omnipresent. When a lightening takes place, it shows us both power and light. It is like a metaphor for the presence of God.

The secret about the appearance of God is understanding the nature of power and light.

Of His Punishment

This chapter deals with a very relevant secret of God. The talk about His 'punishments' will shudder the believers, it will not, however turn on the atheists. Because atheist will believe all the calamities befalling on humanity have scientific or natural reasons. The believers always fear that the God's punishment is not far for wrong doers. This chapter will gather relevant information from holy scriptures and reason it with happenings from oldest known time till today so as to see how the punishment of God was sent to mankind from time to time.

The Old Testament and Quran has many stories of 'punishment of God' for the people who were wrong doers, who denied the messengers or the law of God. They were punished.

Let us begin with Old Testament. *"God shows wrath on his own people, after the law was given, when they violated it.* (Exodus 19). The people of Kind David, 70,000 Israeli were killed as punishment. (Samuel 24:15). The people of Noah were punished and drowned except few God-fearing ones who were with Noah.

People of Prophet Lot were cursed and punished by God for indulging in Sodomy. The Lot's wife 'became a pillar of salt' when she looked back.

The Bible reminds, '*I will punish the world for its evil, and the wicked for their iniquity; I will put an end to the pomp of the arrogant and lay low the pompous pride of the ruthless.*' (Isaiah 13:11).

Jesus was an epitome of love, compassion, and mercy for humanity. '*Let who has not committed a sin in his life throw the stone first*', '*offer the second cheek if someone slaps you*', was his teaching. The punishment and warning concept that prevailed in Old Testament was not as influential in New Testament. The Bible (New Testament) was authored by St. Paul, Mark, John, Mathew and Luke were not among the 12 apostles, nor they did meet Jesus in real life. But all authors were influenced by the fact that Jesus was an epitome of love and compassion for humanity.

There is no mention of God's punishment in Hinduism. It is the concept of *Karma* that will judge a person's good deed and bad deeds for attaining the moksha. (Here Moksha is the cycle of rebirth). It is believed that a person's second birth will be according to his Karma in this life.

The Quran is a book of 'warning, good tidings and guidance' for mankind. All the punishment of God to the people of earlier messengers as narrated in Old Testament are revealed in Quran as well in same or different narrative. 'We meted out a severe punishment to the transgressors because they were rebellious. And then, when they disdainfully persisted in doing what they had been forbidden to do, we said to them, 'Be as apes, despised.' (V7:169). Quran however, has an affirming attribute of God as the most compassionate, forgiving and merciful.

In Quran, God says, *"I will forgive all your sins except Shirk (associating partners to God)." "God is Protecting Friend of those who believe. He bringeth them out of darkness into light."* (V2:257).

In common parlance, earthquakes, cyclones or pandemics are considered as the wrath or fury of God. For an analysis, we hold this belief for the concept of punishment of God as described in holy scriptures through different times and we reason it with many natural disasters that devasted human living in the history of mankind. Is there a link between these two phenomena?

Every natural disaster or epidemic beyond control of humanity such as earthquake, cyclone, Tsunami, or a pandemic is considered as an act of God. The history of humanity has witnessed many such happenings and disasters. The 1964 Great Alaska earthquake was on a Good Friday. More than 4,000,000 died in 1931 China floods. The Spanish flu, the plague of Athens, the pandemic of HIV, all claimed millions of human lives. Shall we consider this as the punishment of God? We find a clear guidance about the punishment of God in Quran, *"And never did We destroy the townships unless the folk thereof were evil-doers."* (V28:59).

Did God punish humanity? Did God destroy cities or wrong doers? This is an important secret of God. An analysis in relation to what is revealed in Old Testament about the wrath or fury of God gives an impression that when angry God is very hard on wrong doers. A verse in Quran says, *"There is only One God. So of Me, Me only, be in awe."* (V16:51)

On the other side of this subject, Jesus was an apostle of love and sweetness. He only spoke about the mercy, favors and kindness of God. Every time a miracle occurred through Jesus, he reminded his people to trust God and His mercy. Quran has many verses telling us that God is merciful, forgiving and compassionate. In fact, an entire chapter is titled, "The Beneficent" in Quran.

In Hinduism, Brahma is Creator, Vishnu is Preserver and Shiva is destroyer.

God is Creator for humanity. And He created everything in this world for the benefit of mankind. God created Adam with 'both His hands' (Quran) and 'breathed His own into his nostrils' (Old Testament). Jesus said God loves His creation. God is all compassionate, merciful and benevolent.

Here we are searching for a secret of God. Is God a destroyer, punisher for humanity or forgiving, merciful, compassionate and benevolent? Or is He both? Holy scriptures are describing both sides. However, there is a verse in Quran that reveals this secret of God explicitly. It says, *"So, remember me and I will remember you,"* (V2:152).

Understanding of this verse makes it simple to determine how God can be punisher, destroyer or forgiving, merciful and benevolent. How? There is a simple truth in here. When God created Adam and asked all angels to bow to him, *Iblis* (Devil), refused. He was not an angel but a Jinn, a powerful entity created by God. God declared him outcast. Iblis requested for time before he would be punished. So, God granted him amnesty for an appointed time and *Iblis* vowed to be an enemy of humanity. Here comes the simple logic in the aftermath. When a believer remembers God, as promised, God too remembers him or she. And if God remembers someone, that person is under the protection, mercy and blessings of God. If people in a city, or community forget God, in turn God too forgets about them and turns away from them. And when the God turns away from a people, *Iblis* comes in. It is like the guard of a bank leaving it unprotected. *Iblis* knows that the subjects are no more in protection of God and he has no fear. *Iblis* has the power to cause destruction, havoc on humanity and that explains how the natural disasters, epidemics and calamities occur. God has warned in scriptures that Satan is an enemy of mankind. Until a nation is in protection of God, Satan is helpless. When God is unhappy with a nation, He simply turns away and Satan takes over the affairs of that nation. This is a secret of God how He is punisher and how He is full of mercy and compassionate for those who remember Him.

God & Devil:

Devil is also known as Satan and Iblis.

In this chapter we will call devil as Satan for easy referral. God and Satan immediately flash two parallel tracks as good or bad. God likes good doers, pious and honest. Satan is working against it. Obviously, Satan is a condemned entity. Yet Satan is very powerful. How come Satan is so powerful that he can reach anywhere within seconds? Who gave him these powers? This is another secret of God. The power and existence of Satan is much debated. Let us find out more about Satan. Why is Satan so powerful when he was condemned by God? Divine scriptures have discussed about Satan in details. The Hebrew Bible described Satan as a fallen angel. He earned disgrace from God when his heart was corrupted and pride took over him. The mighty Angel Lucifer fell from the grace of God and turned into an adversary (Satan). The mighty 'angelic' being was condemned by God, *"I threw you to the earth."* (Ezekiel 28:18).

However, later verses in scripture told that though Satan fell from the grace he maintained his access to heavens (or powers) even after his fall (Job 1:6-12; Zechariah 3:1,2). Satan reached the heaven taking the form of a serpent and this led to the first sin of humanity when he beguiled Adam and Eve.

This narration from Old Testament confirms that Satan was not deprived of his powers. He could turn himself into the form of a snake. And perhaps, that is the only transformation Satan was allowed on earth. This view is also supported with another tradition. When Satan was driven out of heavens, he did not leave alone. A bunch of supporting demons joined him in defiance and these accomplices help him carry out his job against the Kingdom of God. This is what is summarized in Hebrew Bible.

Satan, the Devil figures more prominently in the New Testament and Christian theology. The temptation of Christ is a biblical narrative in the gospel of Mathew, Mark and Luke. The Satan came to Jesus in the Judaean Desert as he was in solitude for 40 days. There Satan visited Jesus thrice and tried to tempt him, seeking compromise on his dedication towards God. Jesus rebuked him every time. For Satan it was like tempting Adam in Paradise. Finally, Satan left disappointed until an opportune time. The incident of temptation of Christ showed how Jesus triumphed over Satan and remained adhered to the God. The incident of 'temptation of Christ' also shows us how keen was Satan to carry out his 'contract' with God. Satan tried even with Jesus Christ to carry out the assigned mission of misleading the humanity. The incident of 'temptation of Christ' also raises a question for the basic Christianity belief that Jesus was the son of God or he was the Avatar of God in the form of a man. If Jesus was son of God or God himself in the form of a man, will Satan dare go to him to tempt him down the wrong paths, knowing well that Jesus was the God? The question needs a rational thinking. A common Christianity perception says that Jesus was a divine being who temporarily became a human being. Even if so, Satan who was in the close proximity of God, he will know very well that Jesus was a divine being and would not dare try tempting him.

According to various apocryphal Old Testament texts and extra canonical texts, Satan fell from the Grace of God when he refused to bow to Adam. The angels were asked to bow to Adam, all obeyed except Archangel Samael, the oldest and most power among the angels of God.

What Quran tells us about Satan?

There are explicit verses about Satan in Quran. And here we also see a common link, the 'pride' of Satan described in Hebrew Bible and Quran. While Old Testament described him as the Mighty Angel who was driven out of Paradise for his growing pride about himself, the Quran has more explicit verses about Satan.

Quran tells us that Satan was not an angel but a 'Jinn'. Quran revealed that God has created mankind and 'Jinn' on earth and kept a hidden veil between His two creations. While Man (Adam) was created out of clay, Jinn was created out of smokeless fire. According to Islamic scholars, God has his own reasons for creating Jinn along with mankind. Or Jinn was created much ahead of creation of Adam. Renowned Islamic scholar Wahiduddin Khan wrote in one of his blogs that, *'He was flying from Istanbul to Mumbai and looking out of window of aircraft and wondering what makes this machine fly in the air? Of course, the Turbo engines sucking the air from front. But was that the engine only or some force employed by God? And he remembered God has created Jinn. May be God assigned Jinn to carry out such hidden jobs?'* Because when God finished creating Adam and breathed unto him, he asked all angels to bow to the Adam. All angels fell in prostration to Adam except Satan, *"He was of Jinn".* (V18:50).

According to Quran, Satan was not an angel, he was a Jinn who enjoyed the privilege of being in close proximity with God. This fact leads to another fact. In modern parlance, it is believed that Angels are like Robots, created to carry out the commands of God. Robots will obey whatever the Master will command them. Angels are like Robots to carry out the commands of God.

God commanded angels to bow to Adam. This is confirmed from both Hebrew Bible and Quran. And all fell in prostration to Adam except Satan. Satan did not obey the command of God because he was not angel, he was Jinn. He was the most powerful Jinn created out of smokeless fire (Quran).

An analysis of disobedience of Satan, as described in Old Testament and Quran, also reveal a secret of God, that He is all forgiving and merciful. Satan had disobeyed the command of God but God did not destroy him. It was in the power of God to turn Satan to ashes the same moment when he disobeyed. But God has reasons. God only banished Satan from His company. God did not destroy Satan but condemned him from Paradise. Satan asked for reprieve and God granted him. Satan asked his

Master to let him do the job of 'beguiling' or misleading the mankind. And God granted him to do so until an appointed time but announced that, *"He will fill hell with Satan and his followers'*. At the same time, God told Satan that he will never succeed in tempting his righteous believers. There, at that moment knowing well the Satanic disobedience for his pride, God was not only assigning him a task with a challenge but also wanted him to realize in the end what He created (Adam) was far above the understanding of Satan. The Old Testament said, *"God has breathed his own into Adam's nostrils"*, Quran said God said to Angels that, *"I am about to create a human being out of clay and when I have formed him fully and breathed My spirit into him, prostrate yourselves before him"*. (V38:71).

Satan, who was the privileged Jinn in the company of God, did not prostrate. He was too proud for being created out of fire and did not like to bow to a creation from clay (Adam). Satan did not realize that God has breathed 'his own' into Adam. And here we have this secret of God, he allowed Satan to take his own time to familiarize himself for His creation of mankind. Both a task and a challenge were given to the Satan. And little Satan did realize that Adam was filled with the 99 traits of God Himself.

An analytical study of holy scriptures reveal that God has warned mankind that Satan is an enemy of men. Repeating for emphasizing that Satan is enemy of Man and not an enemy of a woman! Here, we have another secret of God revealed, that He created man and added some of 'His own' into man.

A woman was created for the comfort of a man. Hebrew Bible tells us that Eve was created from one of Adam's ribs to be his companion. They were living happily in paradise until the Satan starts his mission 'misleading humanity'. Satan enters paradise in the form of a snake and tempts Eve. This incident needs analysis. Satan is allowed to appear in the form of a snake in front of mankind. Perhaps, no other form is allowed to him for appearance before mankind. For this reason, a Muslim is asked to break his prayer if a snake comes in sight, otherwise a praying Muslim cannot break the prayer. There are also hundreds of stories about Jinn appearing as serpent before humanity. Secondly, Satan always find a smoother way to carry out his job. He knows well that a man has few qualities of God within him, so very often he uses a woman for weakening a man. And the history is replete with for this fact. Once the Satan is inside a man, he turns him against humanity. Again, history has many records for this fact. Many men in power massacred humanity. From oldest history of mankind until modern history, the humanity has witnessed Satanic crimes committed by men in power. The Genghis Khan in old times and Hitler, Pot pol, Idi Amin in modern history. They were called 'evil' for their abuse of power, killing innocent humans. But they were not compared to Satan. In reality the rulers like of Genghis Khan and Hitler were actually possessed by Satan. This is another secret about the creation of God. The Satan, originally a Jinn can either appear as a snake in sight or he has the power to enter into the body and minds of a person, called 'possessed'. Once Satan enters into mind and body of a man, the possessed man acts like a devil. Genghis Khan, Hitler, Pol Pot or Idi Amin and many others like of them were possessed by Satan. They oppressed humanity, killed innocent people because the rightly guided men did not check them in time. The Satan does not lose time when he notices a man with hatred for other human being. And if such a person is in authority, the Satan takes over him. Satan will enter into the mind of a ruler immediately when he finds a ruler is nurturing hatred for fellow beings, the ruler who fails to do justice or turns away from justice to his people. Because 'justice' is among the likes of God. When a person indulges in injustice his mind's windows are open for Satan. Satan creeps slowly into the mind of such a person and soon possesses him in entirety. If such a person is a ruler or a man in authority, he commits injustice, atrocities or oppress his subject. The only solution is God fearing people should check him and deprive him power he possesses. Satan will leave such a person when he will see a force of rightly guided people coming against such a 'possessed' man in authority.

The humanity forgot the earliest warning of God, that Satan is an enemy of Man.

God knew the pride and jealousy of Satan towards Adam. Obviously, Satan lost his privilege, position and grace from God, only because Adam(man) was created. But as said in holy scriptures, Satan will be helpless before believing men. He is sent to earth for the 'test' of mankind. He can only tempt such people who are weak in their faith for God or who are not under the guarding sphere of God. In Quran Muslims are promised that "you remember me and I will remember you." The best safety from Satan is under the protection of God. Satan cannot reach or influence God fearing men.

Satan has no enmity with a woman. In fact, he uses woman as the easy tool to reach the mind of a man. This is true from the prime history of mankind, when Satan used Eve for the temptation of Adam. And there were many beautiful women, the history tells us, who destroyed many men of honor. The Cleopatra, the Helen of Troy are few examples. A woman remains the best tool for Satan to mobilize his operation 'temptation' against the men. Satan knows it for 'sure' that a man has one or more of the 99 qualities of God within him. In heaven, he did not approach Adam directly for temptation but worked through Eve. And Satan is keeping the same line of work. And this is yet another secret of God. When God allowed Satan to do the 'temptation' work, He told Satan that he will not influence the God fearing, God believing men. Satan remembers this, and he keeps searching for easy tools, mostly women around stronger men.

God has two reasons for employing Satan.

He wanted to punish him for his pride and disobedience and at also God wanted Satan to live over time and see the wonders of His creation, mankind. In earlier mankind history the job of temptation was easier for Satan. He must have watched the helplessness; hardship of humanity and it must have been a matter of joy for him that humanity was so hard pressed.

He easily did his job. But in modern times, Satan must have been wondering if his powers are any match to mankind? He must have been watching mankind leaving the earth's sphere, walking in space and landing on other planets. For Satan, this is the real slap. He cannot go beyond the gravitation of earth, but mankind has made it possible for themselves. Mankind has reached beyond gravitation of earth, into outer space. Satan must have believed it by now that God created Man more powerful than what he was. And this is the real slap on face of Satan. He is already humiliated, much ahead of time allocated to him. And this is yet another secret of God. Humiliation in this world is a kind of punishment for wrong doers. Satan was proud that he was created by fire and refused to bow to Adam who was created out of clay. Today, Satan must have realized that he has no match to the powers of Adam. Yet, he is carrying out his job.

Satan disobeyed and lost his privilege from the company of God. Yet, he was employed for the mission 'temptation'. His appointment for a fixed time was similar when few governments employee their jail convicts to carry out some risky jobs. And Satan is diligently doing his work along with other demons who left with him from Paradise.

Satan can beguile, tempt or mislead only such persons who are easy targets. Any person who hates other fellow human is easy prey for Satan. Because it was 'hate' for Adam that cost Satan the privilege and company of God. Had he not hated Adam or let us say 'humanity', he would still have been enjoying the proximity of God. God has sensed the 'hatred' in Satan's mind and wanted to keep an open challenge to him. That he will mislead mostly such men who 'hate' others. More the humanity hater, more prone to Satan. In fact, slowly Satan rules the minds and actions of such men. As a result, the world has seen serial killers, rapists, tyrant dictators, all of them possessed by Satan. Humanity haters are turned into dictators or killers of innocent people. Such persons are live example of being possessed by Satan. Satan will not go close to a person who loves humanity or being kind to others. Because such person is God fearing and rightly guided. None of Satanic missiles will harm such a person. Satan has tried this earlier and he was convinced he cannot play around with a man who loves humanity. This happened to him when he tried tempting Jesus Christ. He failed because Jesus was an apostle of love for humanity. A clear guidance is revealed about Satan in divine scriptures. A close study of Satanic history also reveal that Satan is an enemy of men. He is not enemy of women; he is using women as tools for facilitating his job. Satan is helpless against God fearing men, against such humans who like justice and love humanity. Satan will not even go close to such human beings.

It is a myth that Satan will entice each and every human. Satan does not waste his time where he cannot succeed. He avoids such men who remember God, who do justice and love humanity. Such people are vaccinated against Satanic vices. There are also some religious rites that keep Satan out for ever. An Islamic practice is very symbolic for disbanding Satan forever. The Muslim pilgrims hit Satan with stones at three different places during Hajj pilgrimage, where it is believed that Satan tried to tempt Prophet Abraham who was taking his son Ismael for the sacrifice as commanded by God. This act of stoning Satan symbolizes a belief that Satan is condemn and he will not have an influence over the pilgrim in remaining part of his life.

The Hindus too condemn Satan during the annual Diwali festival. An effigy of Ravan (evil) who fought with the virtuous Ram (symbol of goodness) is burnt to celebrate the victory of goodness over the evil. All those participating in burning of Ravan's effigy are destroying the evil.

The relationship between God and Satan are mystic.

It is also not appropriate to call Satan by bad names. He once enjoyed the proximity of God almighty. He was very close to God and he was condemned for his disobedience. At the same time, Satan was assigned a job and he is doing it to the best of his caliber. God has warned in holy scriptures that Satan is an enemy of mankind and it is up to a believer how to keep the Satan away. And there is only one way to do so. Remember and fear God, do justice and love others. Satan will not dare come close to a such a man. Satan could not tempt Jesus Christ because he was an apostle of love for humanity. We also find a reference in the famous sayings of Prophet Muhammad. He was once asked by a companion to give the best advise and Prophet told him, "Love everything God has created". If we analyze this saying of Prophet Muhammad, we may summarize that all those Muslims who hate pigs are influenced by Satan because pig is also a creation of God Almighty. Eating of pork or swine flesh is forbidden in Islam. But no where in Quran or sayings of Prophet, Muslims are advised to dislike or hate the pigs. This deviation in matter of faith generates a kind of 'hate' in mind that opens an inviting window to Satan. A study of Indian sub continents history shows that many communal riots were flared up when miscreant Hindus killed pigs and left the dead bodies on the door steps of mosque. Muslims did not tolerate this and killed the cows and left it at the door steps of temples. This flared up both sides and many innocent lives were lost. The Satanic flare up did havoc on innocents lives for a number of times in the history of Indian subcontinent. Had Muslims simply collected the dead pigs even once without responding violently and dumped it elsewhere, Satan would have been defeated in his professional maneuvering.

The chapter on Satan can be concluded with a final note that Satan is an enemy of men. He is using women as easy tools for accomplishing assigned mission. Satan shies away from a man who is God fearing, love others and do justice. Satan likes someone who is proud, hates others, deny justice. He jumps at such a person and freely enters into his body and soon rules the mind of such a person. And if that person happens to be in authority a dictator like Hitler is reborn.

Will Satan get the respect back? Will Satan get the privilege he lost? Will God forgive him? The answers for these questions are best known to God Himself. But as analyzed in this chapter, God has already punished Satan. It is explicitly evident to

Satan that Man is more powerful. Man can go outside the orbit of earth, into space and unto other planets. Satan cannot go outside the orbit of earth. This humiliation to Satan is the punishment of God. And this reveals a secret to us, that the punishment of God is never far behind.

Fate, Destiny & Age:

Both fate and destiny for a person are commonly considered as predetermined by God.

One's 'fate' and age, is often said to have been set and written at the time of birth. Even it is believed that one's fate is written before birth. What is fate and what does it do to a person throughout his or her life and how is it related to God? It is commonly believed that fate brings fortune or unfortune for humans. While many humans will not believe in 'fate' and stick to reality, majority believe in its existence. Followers of Christianity consider God to the be force behind awarding a fate. It is considered as predetermined. We see in Bible, " *Jeremiah 29:11 - "For I know the plans I have for you," says the Lord. "They are plans for good and not for disaster, to give you a future and a hope."*

Here, the Biblical message is very clear that God has only 'good plans' for the believer.

So how does misfortune befall humans? What causes ill luck? What turns the good plans into bad ones and invites misfortune? The answer is in this Hinduism belief that it is the *Karma* that brings good or bad luck for anyone. The good or bad deeds by a person *(Karma)* earns him good or bad luck. *Karma* alone stands as a milestone for guidance to mankind. And the Quran has a very explicit verse on this subject. Quran says, *"Man shall have only that for which he strives."* (V 54:39). There is another similar verse announcing in clarity that, *"God does not change the condition of a people until they change it themselves."* (viii. 53; xiii. 11). The Command of God is giving a clear verdict that *'man shall have only what he strives for'*. Both these Quranic verses are totally dismissing the concept of 'good or bad luck'. You get what you try for. Again, the verse in very much in line with Hindu philosophy of Karma. Your good or bad deeds will earn you rewards or misfortunes. So, it is obvious that the fate or destiny is not fixed, but it can be achieved. A person has to strive to set his fate or goals.

There is a very famous couplet from Urdu poet Iqbal that reads that *'Raise your eminence so high that before writing a destiny, God will check with you, "What do you want?".* This couplet is very close to a secret of God, that God grants you what you strive for. Even a lottery will not come your way unless you try for it. This secret of God tells us that it is futile to think that a written fate will bring a good or bad destiny. But the fate and destiny always remained a subject of discussion among scholars. Many views and quotes have been written and recorded on destiny. I find this most interesting and relevant. Said by an Arabic scholar, Imam Syafi, *"My heart is at ease knowing that: what was meant for me, will never miss me. And that what misses me, was never meant for me."*

After fate and destiny, comes the factor of 'age'. How is the 'age' of a person determined? Is it predetermined? A common understanding about age suggests that a person lives a life what is fixed for him at the time of birth. There is no medical, scientific or religious support for this view. The religious scripture would not tell us that a man's life is fixed as his fate or destiny. That a person will die only when his or her times come. But there are verses in holy scriptures that tell us about duration of age or old age. Bible tells us, *"The years of our life are seventy, or even by reason of strength eighty; yet their span is but toil and trouble; they are soon gone, and we fly away."* (Psalm 90:10). The Vedas say the average human lifespan is around 100 years. Hindu Vedas says, the average human lifespan is around 100 years.' In real life we see infant dying, young children dying, young men or women dying or very older men dying crossing the age of 100 or above. So how the age factor is allocated?

Quran tells us that *"Every living thing will taste death."* Another verse in Quran about age tells that, *"If we extend anyone's life, We, reverse his development."* (V36:68). Does it mean that the age of a person can be increased or decreased? Another verse in Quran says, **"No person knows what he will earn tomorrow, and no person knows in what land he will die. Verily, God is All-Knower, All-Aware." (V 31:34)**

From olden times we heard a prayer among different religious groups that say, *"May God grant you longer life"*. Do prayers help make one's life longer? Is one's age is predetermined like the fate or destiny? The religious scriptures have vaguely hinted at the age factor. The Quranic Ayat *"If we extend anyone's life."* hints and reveals a secret of God that it is in His power to increase or decrease the life of a person. This also matches with the concept of age-old prayers that, *"May God grant you longer life"*. This also reveals another secret that age of a person is not fixed.

There are numerous scholiastic views that death of a person comes at a fixed hour. A person will die at an appointed hour only and no one can escape from that hour. So, no one can die earlier, unless a person commits suicide or ends his or her life on his own. The famous Muslim army general Khalid Bin Waleed who fought many successful wars with most powerful established empires in history, died of an illness. Just before his death, he spoke to his friends that he does not remember how many wars he fought and how many wounds he had on his body, but he never met with his death in a battle ground and he was dying on a bed due to illness. There are many similar real-life stories about a reality that death of a person occurs at an appointed hour.

But this brings back the same question. Is the age of a person is fixed or it can be increased or decreased? A little more research on this 'age' factor will reveal yet another secret of God. Of course, God has the power to do so, to whom He may give long life and to whom He may give short life but is there a criterion fixed by God? The divine religious scriptures have no say on this line. However, there are hints in some sayings. The Islamic Caliph Ali Bin Talib was quoted as saying, *"Save your rizk (provision) to live longer"*. The Prophet of Islam, Muhammad said, "*A human being fills no worse vessel than his stomach. It is sufficient for a human being to eat a few mouthfuls to keep his spine straight. But if he must (fill it), then one third of food, one third for drink and one third for air.*" Muhammad advised that one should not eat to fill his belly. Leave some space in the belly, that means eat less. In his life, Muhammad was fond of fasting. Every afternoon when he came home from the mosque, he will ask his wife for lunch and if told nothing is cooked at home, he will do fasting.

There are also stories of Hindu saints who wandered in wilderness looking for God. They spent years in solitude. What did they eat? They ate little but lived longer. A secret is revealed here. God has not fixed the age of a person but has fixed his provision. Each person comes to life with a fixed amount of food and he or she lives until the provision is consumed. This is also a medical reality. Eat less and live longer, eat too much and shorten your life span. And this is how God laid his rules. Since God appointed man as his deputy, a man is ultimately working on the designs of God. Eat less and increase the life, eat more and decrease the life.

Among Prophets of God, Prophet Noah's age was recorded at 950 years and youngest Prophet Jesus lived 33 years. Prophet Muhammad died at the age of 63 years. The age and death of Prophet Moses is not known. However, there is an interesting story about his death. When the Angel came to take his soul, he got mad at him and turned him away saying it was not time for him to die. He spoke to God and asked for more time to live. God asked him how many years more he wants? He could not give the numbers then God asked him to count the hairs of sheep standing in front of him and he will be given that many years. At that time, Moses realized that each living soul has to meet the Creator on an appointed time.

In modern history, Guinness World recorded Emilio Flores of Puerto Rico as the oldest living man at the age of 112. Jeanne Calment from France, a woman is also reported to have lived 122 years.

Why different religious faith?

The Creator is One undoubtedly.

But why are there so many religious faiths? There are Jews, Christians, Muslims, Hindus, Buddhists, Zoroastrians, Sikh and so on. There are roughly 4,300 religions all over the world. Christianity and Islam are two widely spread religions. Buddhism, Judaism and Hinduism are other widely professed faiths in the world. There is, however, no evidence that the God of any faith has any clash with the God of other faith. Only the followers clash with each other. Some religious faiths are monotheist and some are polytheist. The Abrahamic faith, Judaism, Christianity and Islam are linked with a basic belief for the same God. These religions are defined as divinely revealed faith. Human history has recorded miracles that occurred during the periods these faiths were revealed. The Messengers conveyed the dictates of God to people. Why the religion was not revealed once only? This question reveals another secret of God. That God planned everything for mankind step by step. Earlier Messengers only asked their people to believe in God and do the right things in life. Moses announced the

Commandments of God and established worship, however the faith remained within the people of Moses.

Jesus reminded people where Moses left. He reminded 10 Commandments and all that Moses taught to his people. This was the second step. The era of Jesus ends and his companions, St Paul, John and Mathew renew his teachings in New Testament. After a gap of 600 years, Muhammad is assigned to renew the same faith. The Quran affirms all Messengers from Abraham to Moses, Jesus, and declares Muhammad as the last Messengers. If we study the link of these 3 faiths, we have a clear guidance. That God wanted to spread His word step by step. It was like teaching from Primary school to high school and finally to university. In Quran we also have this verse, *"To every one of you, We have ordained a law and a way, and had God so willed, He would have made you all a single community. (V5:48)."*

So, God has reasons for spreading different faiths among different regions or nations. But a reality stands supreme that God is the Creator for all and God is ONE. A Jew cannot tell a Christian that he is worshiping the 'right' God nor a Christian can tell to a Muslim that his 'God' is the truth, neither can a Muslim boast that God is for his faith only. This 'my God' feeling or concept is against the will of God. It generates hatred or dislike for the other's faith. We are already watching results. Gone are the days when religion played an important role for the political establishment so there was 'Christian crusades against Muslims. The power game is taken over by hatred. A Hindu feels pride by forcing a helpless Muslim to chant 'Jai

Shri Ram' (meaning Hail the God Ram), slogan. As if Hindu God will earn the respect or status only if a Muslim will chant 'Jai Shri Ram'. This reminds the day when Hitler created a self-edifying slogan, "Hail Hitler." The slogan 'Hail Hitler' was based on hatred against non-Germans. Education and civilization have not mitigated the 'hate game' initiated by Hitler. It is all over the world. Eighty percent of Hindu population in India is easily misled about the possibilities of danger emanating from the eleven percent of Muslims. The white supremist in US keeps frowning against growing population of brown. The Israel has got the entire Holy land in their possession but feels it necessary to uproots few Palestinians from their homes. As if there is no land for the Jews in the kingdom of Israel. Zealot Muslims often target Hindus and Sikh in Pakistan. Why the peace-loving Buddhists suddenly take arms in hand against helpless fellow Muslims in Myanmar? Why religion is generating the 'hate waves' all over the world? This 'why' is very important if we consider the fact that 'Creator' is only One for the entire humanity. The truth is, majority population in any country will not like minorities. The minorities are the bed of thorns for the majority in many countries.

Imagine if there would have been only one language spoken by humanity.

If only one religion practiced by mankind all over the world. The Creator is ONE and it should have happened that way. But it did not happen so because God has reasons and He designed everything in His own ways. All divine religious scriptures were revealed in different languages. The Old Testament in Hebrew, Bible in Greek, Quran in Arabic, Vedas in Sanskrit. Humanity has diversity in each region of the earth. The people of Europe are different than the people of Asian or African countries. Some are white, some are black, some are tall and others are short. And each region has its own culture. The scientific theories define this diversity according to time frame the humanity developed in different regions at different times. But, what about the color of skin? How come the humans are white, black or brown? Science defined the color of skin, hair and eyes as pigment cells 'Melanin' in human body. Science also closed this chapter as the 'Race' or 'Gene'. 'Genes or DNAs are also studied for different races. The science has reasons and explanations.

Here these differences in race, color, languages and religious faiths are guiding us towards another secret of God. *That God likes diversity.* Every nation, race or region is creation of God in diversity. No religion, faith, color of skin or language has any supremacy over the other. It was so conceived, planned and designed by God Himself. But this secret of God, His design for diversity, is the root cause of 'religious conflicts' all over the world. The conflict occurs when a religious group will not accommodate the existence of other faith or overrule the good guidance of its own faith. We have a live example here. A Command of God in Quran tells Muslims that, "This day (all) good things made lawful for you. The food of those who have received the Scripture is lawful for you, and your food is lawful for them." (V 5:5). When Muslims are reminded for this verse, an argument is put forward that People of Scripture (Jews and Christians) are not the same as they were at the time these verses were revealed and they have changed over the time. This view is shared by a majority of Muslims and Islamic scholars as well. No one asks these Muslims or scholars who put this argument that if the People of Book are changed, does this means that when God revealed this verse, did he not know that the People of Book will change over the time? There is no supplementary verse in Quran asking Muslims to be careful and watch out if Jews and Christians are changed. This misunderstanding or self-interpretation of a ruling is the cause of conflict.

While there is little evidence to support that Jews and Christians who lived during pre-Islamic era are different now, except how they were dressed at that time and how they wear now; there is, however, very strong evidence that Muslims are changed over the time. During the time of Prophet Muhammad, they were Muslims only believing in One God and Muhammad as the Messenger of God. Now there are Sunni Muslims, Shia Muslims, Hanafi, Sanbli, Wahabi and so on? Prophet asked Muslims to follow only Quran and his *Sunnah* (sayings and practices of Prophet). Now Muslims follow Imams and different schools of thought. And the new Muslims are all over the world, perhaps, except Saudi Arabia. The Kingdom of Saudi Arabia has upheld the original values of Islam and did not allow adulteration in the faith and its traditions. In other parts of Muslim world, particularly in Indian sub-continent, Muslims identify themselves more as Sunni, Shia, Hanafi and so on. Many Muslim scholars make public appearances not in par with the Sunnah traditions. Prophet of Islam recommended that men shall sport beard and trimmed mustache. Many Muslims, including few scholars, remove mustache completely and keep beard. The four 'rightly guided' caliphs after Prophet used to keep both mustache and beard. Caliph Omer was so careful about his mustache that before going to Friday sermon he will check that no hair of his mustache is coming over his upper lip as he thought his appearance in public should be in accordance with Sunnah. The followers of Islam are changed and diverged from Sunnah but keep claiming that their book brothers (Jews and Christians) are changed.

The fact remains that Islam was 'completed' in the life time of Prophet Muhammed and sealed by God Himself with this verse, "This day I have perfected your religion for you and completed My favor unto you, and have chosen for you as religion Al Islam." (V 5:3). The Prophet also told at the same time that he was leaving behind Quran and his Sunnah (sayings and practices) for guidance. He did not tell Muslims that Imams will come after him for guidance. Majority of Muslims feel that by revealing this verse, God has completed religion of Islam for the entire humanity. The verse is very clear. God is addressing Muslims that religion is perfected and completed for 'you'. A clear guidance misunderstood by many Muslims that undermine tolerance and respect for other faiths. Muslims and scholars tend to forgetting that God announced in Quran, *"And had God so willed, He would have made you all a single community. (V5:48)."* And *"unto you is your religion and unto me is mine.*" Many practices of Prophet Muhammad revealed that he wanted Islam as an 'easy' faith for the followers and had Muslims so adhered, Islam could have guided others for many secrets of God. The secret of God that He preferred 'diversity and secularism' for the humanity is more explicitly discussed in Quran and Sunnah than in any other faith. A single small verse in Quran has a very wider guidance for the entire humanity that, *"had God so willed, He would have made you all a single community."* Another verse, *"In every nation We sent our Messengers"* also guides us to the fact that diversity in faith is the design of God. If God so willed the entire humanity would have embraced a single faith. Like race, color, languages and regions, God has designed diversity on earth and preferred mankind respect each other's faith. We discover these secrets of God that there is beauty and there is diversity in His creation.

Of His Rewards:

There is a very old belief that God rewards whom He likes. God is the king maker. God awards honors and status to whom He chooses. His rewards are plenty but not recorded in mankind history. What are the selection criteria? Religious scholars have spoken on this topic and pointed few choices that could earn rewards from the God, almighty. The priests, clerics and Maulvis have declared that God rewards for faithfulness, devotion, belief, service, sacrifice or those diligently seeking Him. All true. Religious scriptures also tell that God rewards for good deeds. It is said in old Bible, *"Whatever you do, work at it with all your heart as working for the Lord, not for human masters, since you know that you will receive an inheritance from the Lord as a reward."* (Colossians 3:23-24).

Hindus believe that human beings can create good or bad consequences for their actions and might reap the rewards of action in this life or in rebirth. The same is announced in Quranic verses, *"We shall reward them according to the best of their deeds (Q 29:7)." "That God may give them the best reward of what they have done and give them more out of His grace (Q 24:38)."* These verses show that God rewards for good doers.

In human history who were the chosen one rewarded by God? What is the best reward awarded to any person by God? Making a man king from the pauper or giving a hidden treasure? Or wealth or knowledge in this world? Or, are the rewards of God reserved for the life to come? The answer to all these questions reveals another secret of God. The top-ranking award from God for any person is 'honor' in this world. If we ask a simple question to 10 people, as to who the second president of United States was, perhaps eight will not give correct answer. But if we ask same group of 10 who was Thomas Edison, the same 8 will answer, he invented electric bulb. Thomas Edison, Graham Bell, Albert Einstein, Isaac Newton, Wright Brothers, Galileo Galilei, and many others who earned respect and honors, who were exalted in human history because they invented or discovered something to make human life better. Their good work is acknowledged in a divine way. The respect and honor they achieved is ever lasting. Mahatma Gandhi and Martin Luther King also earned respect for caring for humanity. On the other side Adolf Hitler, Genghis Khan, Idi Amin, Pol Pot also impacted humanity but they earned no respect. Everlasting respect and honor are bestowed upon to whom God is pleased and whom God has chosen. These selected among mankind are guided and helped by God for their destiny. And they achieved it. This is yet another secret of God that He rewards respect as the most selected award to few in this world only. This takes back to the Vedic concept that it is 'Karma' that earns good or bad for a person in this life or in life to come after. A verse in Quran affirms this, "O God, Owner of Sovereignty, you give sovereignty to whom You will and You take sovereignty away from whom You will. You honor whom You will and You humble whom You will. (V3:26).

Revealed as a secret, 'respect' or 'honor' remain the top award or reward by God; but there are other rewards noted and recorded in human history. What are these rewards by God for people and how are these given? Does a man is preferred by God for the rewards or a woman is included as well? The religious scriptures, traditions, edicts speak 'whoever' will do a good work will be rewarded. A man or a woman is not specified. However, the honor and respect achievers' list in the history of mankind has mostly men in it.

Of Doomsday:

Even atheists have an inkling of what is the doomsday. That the world will end one day. When and how it will end, nobody knows. This knowledge is with God only. But somehow, this secret is also revealing. The world has already witness Covid 19 onslaught that brought the entire mankind on a standstill. Now many believe it was a trailer for the Doomsday. Whether it was an act of nature or a satanic motivation, the humanity of this age has witnessed what helplessness and devastation will be in store if God turns away and leaves the humanity on its own. The concept of 'doomsday' is both ancient and recent at the same time. It was always talked about in awe and it is now spoken by many, as a reminder for what is coming. The religious scriptures have only announced that world will end. There will be a doomsday and it will come for sure. A verse in Bible says, *"But concerning that day and hour no one knows, not even the angels of heaven, nor the Son, but the Father only."* (Mathew 24:36)

Judaism also believes in the apocalypse and coming of Messiah and resurrection of the dead. A belief that is very close to Islam as well.

It is believed in Hinduism that the world will end and at that time the god Vishnu will come as Kalki at the last hour, riding on a horse and holding a sword similar to a comet. He will destroy the forces of evil.

In Christianity, the Bible's Book of Revelation too speaks about a battle between the forces of God and the Satan called as - the final Armageddon.

Zoroastrians also believe that very few good people will remain on the right path and evil ones will outnumber the good. The Wise Lord (Ahura Mazda) will finish the evil for a Great Renewal at the end of the present age.

The Quran calls doomsday as the *'hour sure to occur but the knowledge of that is with the God Almighty only.'* However, there are descriptions what could be the doomsday and what will happen on that day. That the earth will asunder apart, the mountains will crash like 'running sand'. "My Lord will blow them away with a blast. And He will leave it (i.e., the earth) a level plain. (Quran 20:105).

All divine religious scriptures and beliefs affirm that there will be doomsday and it will be the end or annihilation of the earth. When will it occur? God only knows about it. But surely it will happen. When we think about doomsday or the last day of the earth, a simple perception takes form that God will finish the world. All believers in God believe that doomsday will happen and this beautiful world will meet an end. However, a question pops up. Will the God, all merciful and benevolent who created this world, burst it apart on the doomsday? God has created this world for the humanity. God is loving and kind and He created innumerable bounties for the humankind. What God has created on planet earth is available nowhere else. Not on any other planet in our universe. But as God decreed, every living thing shall taste death, He will bring an end to this world. But how? Some believe that a bang will tear the world into pieces, and some believe that a bang will cause earth lose its rotation on its axis and either the earth will collide with the sun or fall into space losing the warmth of sun. These are the two perceptions widely accepted about the doomsday. But this will not happen until God chooses to do so. Until God has decreed that doomsday will come. We have studied how God planned everything in creating this universe for the mankind. We have also studied how God created man with both His hands. Quran tells us that 'God has appointed Man as His deputy on this earth'. And we all know what are the functions of a deputy. He does everything in the absence of the Chief. So, here we have another secret of God. That the 'man' is performing many duties assigned by God on this planet. Let us be emphatic that a man is the Deputy of God on earth, not a woman. Whenever and wherever a Satanic act appears against humanity, man is guided by God for countering it. The world has witnessed how Covid 19 pandemic brought the world to a standstill. Some believed the pandemic was a result of a careless negligence, while others believed it to be a Satanic act. God fearing people prayed for safety. And scientists soon developed a vaccine for prevention. The vaccines have conquered the pandemic all over the world. God did not send vaccine boxes through angels. But the 'Deputy' of God worked on his own for creating relief to the humanity. The phenomenon that 'man' is performing the assigned duties is witnessed off and on throughout the human history. When Satan possessed Hitler and he committed atrocities on innocent humankind, attacked unprovoked neighbors and plundered many cities, God did not send angels for stopping the Satanic Hitler. But America with allies countered Hitler and finished him as the God will finish Devil. There are many such examples in human history telling us how the man defeated or finished a Satanic possessed person. Satan is at work with all his accomplices possessing many misguided men; but everywhere he is defeated by the men of God. This secret of God that man is working as the Deputy of God has its historical authentication. The Messengers or Prophets of God were not the men of miracles, but they were designated to be so, exhibiting the powers to people of their times as a token that it will be within the power of men to do so. The Man as the assigned deputy of God, will have the power to do so. If we look back in history at the miracles of Jesus Christ there is enough to believe that he was bestowed with divine powers. He restored sight to blind, cured deceased persons, gave life to death. All of his miracles were the tokens that a day will come when men will do the same. Today, doctors can pump the dead heart back to life, restore sight to a blind person by a donor's eyes. The medical research has already isolated many pandemic diseases. All these facts point to this secret of God, that He assigned man as His deputy for performing many tasks in this world.

The secret that the man is assigned by God to perform on His behalf also unfolds the fact of how the world will meet its end on doomsday. The President of the United States of America has the power to push the buttons of nuclear arsenal. The President Harry Truman law gives this power to each elected President. The President does not need a second opinion. The Defense secretary has no say, the US congress cannot interfere. This sole power enables the President of United States to unleash a nuclear war. And what a nuclear war would mean to this planet? Devastation beyond comprehension. The earth could lose its axis and move away. It will either strike the sun or will burst asunder. The Quran describes the scene of doomsday in short verses that mountain will run like sand, the earth will burst apart and sun will come closer. All of this is possible by acts of man, the deputy of God.

Doomsday will happen and bring an end to this beautiful world as decreed by God. But the mankind will be responsible for the destruction of this world. God is very kind and benevolent and it is far from His Grand Mercy that He will punish humanity, His own creation, His most loved and the beautiful world that He created for humans.

This secret of God that He designated Man on earth as His deputy and assigned Man to perform some of His own tasks is phenomenal with live examples everywhere. These assigned men are fighting against every evil. They are judges working in courts, social activists, human right activists, good rulers who care for their people, riches who love charity, doctors who care for saving a human life. All these characters are set by God and He has infused their hearts in such a way that Satan may not dare tread on their ground. On the other side, as discussed in earlier chapters, we have Satan, devil or Iblis ready to harm the humanity in any way. A person who nurtures hatred in his heart for another person for any reason is an easy target for Satan. When Satan comes across a person whose heart is filled with 'hatred' for fellow human, he immediately possesses him and ignites the hatred in his mind and heart and once ignited, this hatred keeps burning, building up. Satan also helps such a person to acquire power and means to spread the fire of hatred all around and we have witnessed such 'possessed' characters in the role of Hitler, Genghis Khan, Idi Amin, Pol Pot and so on. God had planned that man shall defeat the Satan who is an enemy of mankind because Satan hated the humans. If it were not for this plan, God would have burned Satan to ashes the very moment he revolted against Him. But God has destined Satan to be insulted by man. If Satan creates an Hitler against humanity, the army of God loving, God fearing men is always there to counter him. The role of Satan is always described in a one-track narrative by all religious scholars. Religious scholars mostly tell us that Satan is tempting humans for committing sins. And the sins are described as theft, adultery, lying, keeping away from worship and vices so on. But in reality, Satan is on prowl looking out for his targets who can harm the humanity. The moment Satan come across such a person, he creeps unto him and from then Satan is the controller of that man or woman. Satan does not come close to a God-fearing person. A person whose heart is kindled by the light of faith of God is in auto protection from Satan. Satan will helplessly watch such a person or move away from him.

The doomsday or the end of the world will be avoided until such time as the army of God-fearing men will stand against the people possessed by Satan. Once the 'possessed' people will out number the good people, the doomsday will happen as decreed by God. This world will end but God, as He promised in divine scriptures, will arrange transportation of people He liked most, perhaps to another world, more beautiful, more comfortable than this planet. All the evil doers, the Satanic possessed persons, the humanity hater including Satan himself will perish with this world.

Conclusion

There are many faiths and believers in One God all over the world. They could be Zoroastrians, Jews, Christians, Muslims, Hindus and so others. God is accepting worship and prayers from all those He liked. His promise that He will reward to all those who believe in Him is announced in a verse in Quran that says, *"Lo! Those who believe and those who are Jews and Christians and Sabaeans – whoever believeth in God and the Last Day and doeth right, surely their reward is with their Lord."* (Surah 2, V62). This verse in Quran stands as a mile stone in the path of all religious faiths and at the same time stands as a mirror to many hardliner Muslims who think that only Muslims will enter the Paradise. This Quranic verse has emphasized the strongest belief of "Karma" in Hinduism one of the oldest religions. 'Karma' warns us that God will finally judge you for all your actions in this life; you reap what you sow. And once again, a secret of God is reemphasized here; that God will reward for good deeds and punish 'evil' doers. The 'evil' is anything that is against humanity because 'evil' is synonymous with Satan. Here is a warning to humanity haters, or all such persons who hate others for their faith, color, race or language, that they are in the monitoring eyes of God and a punishment will come to their 'evil actions' sooner or later.

The Last Secret of God:

Having studied few relevant secrets of God in this work and arriving at a conclusion that believers in God worship him under umbrellas of different faiths and that He will accept worship and prayers from whom He likes, a question raises. Did God favor any faith or followers of any faith over the others? A reference from Old Testament tells us that, God preferred Jews. In Chapter, Deuteronomy 7:6, God declared the people of Israel as holy, chosen to be *"a people for Himself, a special treasure above all the peoples on the face of the earth." And very interestingly, a verse in Quran also speaks about Jews as preferred people, "O Children of Israel, remember My favor which I have bestowed upon you, and how I preferred you above all other people." (SII, V 122). Since both the divine revelations speak about Jews as the preferred people by God, we need to explore the reasons why Jews were preferred by God. The entire humanity is the creation of God. And throughout this work we have noticed that God loves His creation. His Love for the humanity is like the love of a Father, among humans, for all his children. The Jews were descendants of Prophet Abraham who taught them about One God. The History of Jews from Prophet Abraham till Prophet Moses has many ups and down recorded for them. They were slaves under the rule of Pharaoh when Moses was assigned by God for the mission of their emancipation and Exodus from Egypt. Moses*

brought them to Holy land and advised them to obey God and be blessed or he prophesized that they will be cursed if they did not obey the Lord. The years of persecution of Jews and their exile to different lands were remembered as the 'curse of Moses'. The Quranic verse only reminded Jews that they were the 'favored' people once upon a time but they lost the 'favor' as they incurred a 'curse'. Now Jews, got the 'God promised land'. This promised land was recorded in Old Testament and Quran as well. But Jews may no longer claim to be the 'preferred nation' of God.

Then who among the divine faith are favored by God? Christians enjoyed power and kingdoms all over the world. They were bestowed with education and prosperity. In a way, yes, they were blessed by God as Jesus always prayed for his followers. Jesus even did not curse those who deceived him or tied the cross on his neck. It is said that when Jesus was paraded through the streets of Jerusalem with cross over his shoulder, Angel Gabriel walked along with him and conveyed the message from God if Jesus would like a punishment for the people who wronged him. But Jesus asked for their forgiveness.

Hindus and Zoroastrians enjoyed vast empires and civilizations in early history. The traces of Hindu civilization and kingdoms are recorded in history. The Hindu saints who walked bare feet in wilderness searching for proximity with God, were rewarded with His presence. From ancient till modern times, 'knowledge' was bestowed upon Hindus. Great scholar Swami Vivekananda and humanity crusader Mahatma Gandhi were Hindus.

Islam spread like a fire of faith and Muslims enjoyed power, empires, and prosperity. It is recorded that Prophet Muhammad always prayed to God for mercy and blessing to his followers. Like Jesus, Prophet Muhammad also did not curse his worst enemies. He did not curse even those who hit him with stones or laid thorns in his way. And truly, God answered Prophet Muhammad's prayers. If we study the favors of God to Muslims, we see there are plenty. The Arabs of Middle East who could hardly afford a lunch of few dates or a dry piece of bread, once upon a time, are now wealthiest nations in the world. Qatar, Saudi Arabia and other GCC countries are examples. There are about 50 countries with Muslim majority population in the world. Islam is second largest practiced religion over taking Christianity. Obviously, these are favors for Muslims. But we are looking for a favor bestowed upon Muslims which has not been granted to followers of any other faith. Yes, Muslims have been granted a special favor and this we count as the last secret of God. What is the special favor bestowed upon Muslims? It is the ordinance from God asking Muslims to stay away from consumption of Alcohol and gambling. "They ask you, (O Prophet), about intoxicants and gambling. Say, 'There is great sin in both although they have some benefit for people: but their harm is greater than their benefits.' (Quran, Sur II, V219).

It is well known how alcoholic drinks affect brain, liver and health of a person. Alcoholic drinks were not forbidden in earlier divine religions, so this ordinance is a favor from God for Muslims. Health is more important than anything else for a person. And yet Muslims are not deprived of the benefits of these fermented drinks. Now, non-alcoholic Beer and wine are popular drinks in modern Muslim world. Another favor to Muslims, they are mandated five times daily prayers, a light physical exercise that helps part of body and brain. The worship is for God but the benefits are for believers who perform it 5 times in a day. Another favor from the God is the ordinance for washing of face, hands and feet before each prayer. This is yet another healthy action and now adopted by many non-Muslims as the Covid 19 prevention methods. Muslims are also mandated fasting for a month in a year. The benefits of fasting are widely discussed in modern medical world. This ruling from God is also a favor to Muslims for their healthy well-being. Muslims are also forbidden eating pork meat. Circumcision of male boys soon after birth is also mandated and considered essential for health and hygiene, though it was also prescribed for Jews and Christians. Muslim men are allowed to keep 4 wives but advised to do justice among all. Muslim women are allowed to take divorce if they are not happy with their partners. The contract of marriage and divorce is simplified so as to match the human nature. If we analyze these favors from God to Muslims, we may conclude that the count of favors of God to Muslims is certainly more than favors bestowed upon Jews or Christians. Why so? Jews got only the promised land. That was the promise from God. Christians and Muslims got number of favors. Why? The history of Messengers reveals the facts and reasons. Prophet Moses knew that his people may dither away from the Commands of God and he warned them. Jesus always prayed for the blessings of God for his followers. Prophet Muhammad always prayed for mercy and bounty of Lord for his followers. And we have the results for analysis and here, we get yet another secret of God. God granted what the Messengers and Prophets prayed to him. History has recorded that Prophet Moses was not always happy with his people and he kept warning them. Prophet Jesus was a man with a heart filled with love for humanity. He was kind even for those who ditched him. The same was noted with Prophet Muhammad.

And both prayed for the bounty of Lord for their followers. And God Almighty has answered their prayers. God has showered his mercy to Christians and Muslims. However, this is not the last secret. Time and future will reveal more secrets of God.

Let us focus on an obvious and much ignored secret of God that has unfolded in this work. And this secret is all revealing as to how the God has planned doomsday. That the men misled by Satan or rather possessed by Satan will be responsible for all the calamities and destruction on humanity or cause the doomsday. The earth will perish and so will Satan, since he is confined within the limits of earth only. Let it be known that Satan is always on the lookout for such men who hates others. As soon as Satan comes across such a person, he possesses him and controls his mind and body. Such Satanic possessed persons are enemies for humanity and must be identified and isolated like contagious diseases.

There is a simple protection from Satan.

Believe in God.

Love humanity and everything God has created, and Satan will dare not come in your way. Hatred for others is a cancer for the brain and it will be an open invitation to Satan. Check for its symptoms, treat it and the world will survive and doomsday will be delayed.

The End